ANOTHER PRAYER BOOK

FOR BUSY PEOPLE

Compiled by `Bola John

AKIN-WURA Publishers
Chicago, Illinois

DEDICATION

to the

third millennium of

Christianity

ACKNOWLEDGEMENT

My gratitude goes to God and to all those who have helped me on my way especially the Archbishop of Lagos - Anthony Olubunmi Okogie, the Daughters of Charity, Washington D.C., the Our Lady of Apostles sisters, Lagos; the priests of the Society of African Missions, Lagos; the Society of Jesus, Lagos; the Missionaries for Africa, Chicago and Washington D.C., especially Fr. Abdon Gamulani and Fr. J.G. Donders of the Washington Theological Union; the Archdiocese of Lagos, and finally, Opus Dei members especially Fr. James Chapuli, Lagos. Thanks also to many other good people especially to teachers and friends among whom my late parents, Edward and Mary John are foremost.

There are many others to thank, many of whom have passed away but have left us their words and experiences to share - which have been the enrichment of the author of this book.

Thanks also to Wendy Petzall and Rachel Newton of Manchester, U.K. who helped with the preparation of the manuscript and Andrea Bettinardi, Chicago, who designed the front cover.

Finally, thanks to all who find this book useful and are sharing it with their friends and acquaintances.

FOREWORD

Prayer is the life of a child of God on earth. It is what animates and makes us alive to Him. Prayer is like the beating of the heart. Anyone that neglects his prayer life might be regarded as dead to God. Yet, we very often tend "to forget Him who is our life and our all." (Catechism of the Catholic Church, 2697).

However, prayer cannot be left to a spontaneous outpouring of a momentary "inspiration". We must learn to pray. This means that we must learn to raise our minds and hearts to God, discuss or dialogue with Him. Prayer comes out freely and constantly in our daily life, or while working, resting or moving around in a car, bus or train. The scriptures and the Church's Liturgy are full of examples of 'prayer'. This shows us its importance. But some still find it difficult to pray.

A look at the Scriptures shows that Christ's apostles, learn to pray from Jesus Himself. He taught us to address God as our Father. As we turn our gaze to Him, who is our model, we find clues to his behavior. Before He started His apostolic mission He retired to the desert for forty days and forty nights to pray (cf. Matt. 4: 2). He prayed before He chose His twelve apostles. The Scriptures has it that he went up the hills to pray and "all night He continued in prayer to God" (Luke 6: 12). We read also that before most of His miracles, the Lord Jesus would lift his eyes to heaven and pray (cf. John 11: 41). In fact, the more familiar we are with the Gospels, the more we realize that He was in constant conversation with his Father and that the Holy Spirit inspired all His actions.

To learn how to pray, we must be humble and be aware of our inability to do so for it is the Holy Spirit who "helps us in our weakness: for we do not know how to pray as we ought, but the Spirit Himself intercedes for us with sighs too deep for words" (Romans 8: 26).

The author of this little work has put down things in the simplest form for us to make prayer easy. It is a good aid to keep the heart of the busy working man or woman beating, while helping one at the same time to live in contemplation and child-like trust of our loving Father who cares constantly for us.

I congratulate the author and recommend its use to all.

+A.O. Okogie
Archbishop of Lagos
4th June, 1999

CONTENTS

INTRODUCTION:
WHAT IS PRAYER?

Prayer is the raising up of our being to God, the origin of man, our alpha and omega. It is expression of our faith in God. It is not just reciting words (Matt. 15: 8; Mark 7: 6) but it involves our heart - our capacity to love - directed at God in solemn friendship. We can pray vocally by audible words (formulas or spontaneous words) said or sung; or with our body as we see when Moses raised his hands up with the staff of God (Exodus 7: 11), and David danced (2 Samuel 6: 14,21) or simply in the spirit beyond words (Romans 8: 26; Eph. 6: 18; John 4: 23-24) and thus we can present ourselves conveniently before God in different manners from the simple, charismatic, exuberant bodily prayer to the silent, contemplative form of the spirit - with or without words. Thus every man is capable of prayer.

Without prayer, we lack authentic focus for life and fear death. Prayer, an acknowledgement of God for what He is and what He does, should be, for a healthy soul, constant - like the beating of the heart or like breathing. "Never cease praying" says St. Paul (1 Thess. 5: 17).

The more we know God, the better and more constant our prayer. Jesus came to help us know God and has taught us how to pray by His life (Matt. 11: 25-26; Matt. 14: 23-24; Mark 1: 35; Luke 6: 12) and teaching (Matt. 6: 9-13; Luke 11: 2-4; Luke 11: 5-11; John 14: 13; 16: 23-28). He gave us conditions for effective and pleasing prayer (Matt. 4: 10; Mark 11: 22-25; Mark 14: 36; Luke 11: 1-13; Luke 22: 42) and even enjoined us to use His Name (John 14: 13; 16: 23-28). He taught us to pray to God as Our Father and to make petitions (Luke 11: 5-11). Many of the lessons of Jesus Christ are lessons on prayer. The human race cannot survive without prayer.

Prayer is needed for sanity of mind and sanctity of spirit. Through prayer we can reach beyond natural potentials and natural knowledge (science). We can harmonize our lives with mysteries of existence especially death, destiny, and the origin and end of the cosmos. Through prayer, we put the talents, time, skills, education, experience, social status, money - that God has given us to optimal use and our work and service produce eternal fruits ("fruits that will last" John (15: 16)). Through prayer we gain the power to direct well all our faculties - memory, understanding, will, imagination, emotions, senses and feelings. Through prayer we nullify temptations and do not offend God by thoughts, words, deeds and omissions.

Saint Paul says , "We do not know how to pray as we ought" (Rom. 8: 26). The lack of prayer is the source of human confusions and social problems because God, the origin of man, is the only source of objective truth and morality. Through prayer we discern the end of everything in our lives, in society and in events of time; we sort out values and unite ourselves to God and the path of glory.

God answers all prayers to Him (Romans 8: 32) whether we know it or not. As time advances, prayer is ever more relevant to human life, both as a personal act and as a social act. Without prayer modern liberalization would be reckless, our sense of purpose would be distorted, grasp of the unknown would be frustrating, and the progress of human reason and industry would be catastrophic. Rational philosophy can never adequately replace original human spirit. Human beings cannot be independent of God to a good end. Human will cannot alter the will of God but can be elevated to it and this is the essence of prayer. Lack of prayer ultimately leads to idolatry - the replacement of God with something else or with nothing. We humans continually tend towards idolatry, actively, passively, positively or negatively.

The modern person tends to seek self; to believe only in self; and to esteem self. There is disorderly exaltation of industry and money; fun and sex; and the worship of God may be replaced by fanaticism, addiction or by Satanism without qualm or reserve. There is also the insult of people attributing the works of God to another and blaspheming against the love of God through high-

brow philosophy just like the old case of "Beelzebub" (Luke 12: 10). We cover up the need for relationship with God by intellectual humanism, by executing self-sufficiency, and by the settlement of conscience in philanthropy. We commonly forget or ignore God (Luke 12: 9) and there is also the downright betrayal by people chosen by God (Mark 14: 21; Luke 17: 1). Finally, there abound people who refuse to give God what belongs to Him or what he deserves. Such is seen in the bold atheism, comfortable agnosticism and smug skepticism of today's "progressive society". Christians should not be intimidated by all this into dropping prayer.

Prayer is a source of strength (Luke 21: 34-36); a sure defense and protection (Mark 14: 38; Luke 22: 40; Luke 1: 37) and a great weapon (Matt. 26: 52-53; Mark 9: 29). Through prayer we present our needs to God (Phil. 4: 6). Through prayer we achieve the impossible (Mark 10: 27) and everything in our life is profitable (Luke 12: 31). Above all, through prayer we discover the truth in the assurance of Jesus, "The kingdom of God is within you" (Luke 17: 21). No wonder the devil is actively keeping us from praying.

This book is a little support intended to be a springboard to help personal prayer. It is not a duplication of popular traditional prayer books. It is an addition to the Christian's library, which should already have the Gospel, the Missal, the Catechism and other treasures of Our Faith. It is not intended to teach us how to pray. It is intended to be a help for living in the presence of God at work, on our journeys, in the park, anywhere and in everyday life; and to be equally an accompaniment on holidays and support for spiritual retreats. The book is a small compilation of prayers of Christians of all times, extracts from writings of the Saints, from the Liturgy of the Catholic Church and from Sacred Scripture. "Lord, teach us to pray!" (Luke 11: 1). He has taught us: "When you pray say, 'Our Father'...". The best way to pray therefore is to pray as Children of God.

 MORNING OFFERING 

Our first thought each day should be of God from Whom we came and Who determines our life. The morning offering helps us to identify ourselves with Him and with His Will – the only way to find the true happiness and progress proper to human life. The morning offering could be a simple sentence such as, "Lord I offer You everything" or a formula as is found in many prayer books. The formula below is simply an aid. The first six lines suffice.

O My God,
Through the Immaculate Heart
Of Mary, my Mother,
And the intercession of all the
Angels and Saints in Heaven
I offer You EVERYTHING.
In union with the Holy Mass
Throughout the world,
I give You MYSELF:
My freedom and potencies,
My thoughts, words and deeds;
My acts of piety and work,
My struggles, tendencies,
Dispositions and reactions;

My joys and sorrows, my resolutions;
My time, energy, talents and capabilities,
My sacrifices and rest;
All You have given me and
All that happens to me.
Help me to give You my best in Everything,
With increasing FAITH, HOPE, CHARITY,
GRATITUDE AND CONTRITION
That I may be increasingly
JUST in Your sight,
According to the Truth of Your Gospel.
Use me Lord for whatever You will:
For the Coming of Your Kingdom,
For the perseverance of my brethren;
The happiness of others,
Conversion of those
Who live in sin, error, and ignorance,
Sanctification of souls,
The spreading of Your Gospel;
For the rights and triumphs
Of Your Holy Church
To the Glory of Your Most Holy Trinity.
Make me know Your Will in all Things
And to receive it with a ready FIAT.
In the Name of Jesus,
I plead for graces and merits

Throughout this day
For the Holy Father, the Bishop and
All who hold and teach the Catholic Faith,
For new converts and new vocations,
For my family,
And the whole Church including myself.
Grant me indulgences for my sins Lord
And for the Holy souls in Purgatory.
Give me many opportunities
To correct my failings
And those of others.
Help me to grow in all the virtues
And to heroic degrees.
Make me humbler still,
Detached from everything
And firmly attached to You so that
I MAY DECREASE
And YOU MAY INCREASE in me.
A pure and contrite heart create in me,
O God.
Put a steadfast spirit within me.
O wash me more and more from my sins
And never deprive me of
YOUR HOLY SPIRIT. Amen.

Immaculate Heart of Mary, Pray for us.

PRAYER TO THE GUARDIAN ANGEL
O Angel of God,
My Guardian Dear,
To whom God's Love
Commits me here,
Ever this day
Be at my side
To light
To guard
To rule
And guide. Amen.

 # DAILY PRAYER 

Every day we should find some time to spend quietly with God, to consider our life before Him and ask for graces.   We should make acts of love, adoration, praise, thanks, contrition and reparation. We should speak to him in our minds about our struggle to be pleasing to Him; about the affairs of the Church, the Pope, the Parish, our Christian fellowships and associations; about our families, and friends. We should talk to him about things related to our professional work, events of our times, our personal affairs and the targets for the day.   We should make ourselves attentive to the inspirations and lights He sends us and to the demands He makes on us.   We can pray with our own words or with popular prayers. We should use the Gospel or some approved book to meditate on some aspect of the Christian way of life especially by contemplating the life and teachings of Our Lord Jesus Christ and the elaboration of His way given to us by the lives and teachings of the Saints.   Apart from our personal prayer, we may take part in social prayer especially by praying with our immediate family and with the entire family of the Church by participating in Holy Mass.

 # USE OF TIME 

"Time is a treasure with which we buy our eternity": so said Blessed Josemaria. This has been the feeling of many saints and should be the feeling of those aspiring for sanctity. Time has to be managed well for it to yield such a colossal profit. Every Christian therefore should be determined on the management of time for acts of piety as well as common family, social and professional occupations. Once a timetable or a plan is made, the effort to keep to it is itself virtue engendering. Once we fall into the good rhythm of a timetable well kept, the order maintained allows for a steady progress in the interior life as well as a quicker detection of any bent towards laziness, forgetfulness, negligence or lukewarmness.

In this chapter are suggestions of pious norms of Christian tradition that may be placed in the timetable of a catholic who aims for the highest as far as possible, if the person has no commitment towards more specific acts of piety. We may carry out some daily and others periodically (weekly, monthly or occasionally). It is useful to keep a confidential chart or diary that reflects our faithfulness in keeping up the ascetic struggle and to discuss it with a suitable spiritual director.

DAILY NORMS
Morning offering
Prayer
Holy Mass
Spiritual reading
Angelus
Holy Rosary
Apostolic witness
Charity
Mortification
Examination of conscience

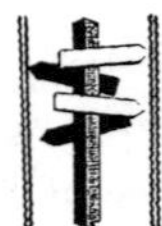

PERIODIC NORMS
Sacramental confession
Spiritual direction
Bible study
Doctrinal classes
Pious fellowship
Spiritual retreat
Works of Mercy
Pilgrimage
Evangelization

POPULAR PRAYERS

As human beings we have imagination, memory, emotions, passions, temperaments, and aspects of behavior, which disturb our ability to pray and very often we need external aid to our interior prayer. When the Apostles asked Jesus to teach them how to pray, Jesus gave them a formula, the OUR FATHER. We all need formulas and guides in order to pray well and we all have a lot to gain from the experiences of the Saints.

OUR FATHER
Our Father,
Who art in heaven,
Hallowed be thy name.
Thy Kingdom come.
Thy will be done
On earth as it is in heaven.
Give us this day our daily bread,
And forgive us our trespasses,
As we forgive those
Who trespass against us.
And lead us not into temptation,
But deliver us from evil.
Amen.

HAIL MARY

Hail, Mary, full of grace;
The Lord is with thee,
Blessed art thou among women,
And blessed is the fruit of thy womb, Jesus.
Holy Mary, Mother of God,
Pray for us sinners, now,
And at the hour of our death. Amen.

GLORY BE TO THE FATHER

Glory be to the Father,
And to the Son,
And to the Holy Spirit.
As it was in the beginning,
Is now, and ever shall be,
World without end. Amen.

THE APOSTLES' CREED

I believe in God,
The Father almighty,
Creator of heaven and earth,
And in Jesus Christ
His only son our Lord;
Who was conceived by the Holy Spirit,
Born of the Virgin Mary;
Suffered under Pontius Pilate,

Was crucified, dead and buried;
He descended into hell;
The third day he rose again from the dead;
He ascended into heaven,
And is seated at the right hand
Of God the Father almighty;
From thence he shall come
To judge the living and the dead.
I believe in the Holy Spirit;
The holy Catholic Church;
The communion of saints;
The forgiveness of sins,
The resurrection of the body,
And life ever lasting. Amen.

THE CONFITEOR

I confess to almighty God
That I have sinned through my own fault,
In my thoughts and in my words,
In what I have done,
And in what I have failed to do;
And I ask Blessed Mary ever virgin,
And all the angels and saints,
To pray for me to the Lord our God. Amen.

ACT OF FAITH
My God, I believe in you
And all that your Church teaches,
Because you have said it,
And your word is true. Amen.

ACT OF HOPE
My God, I hope in you,
For grace and for glory,
Because of your promises,
Your mercy and your power. Amen.

ACT OF LOVE
My God, I love you above all things,
Because you are so good yourself;
Teach me to love you daily more and more.
Amen.

ACT OF CONTRITION
O my God, because you are so good,
I am very sorry that
I have sinned against you
And by the help of your grace
I will not sin again. Amen.

 # PRAYERS FOR OTHERS 

We should not strive for our own sanctity alone and expect to reach Heaven. We have to pray for others; for the Church (Eph. 6: 18; Col. 4: 2-4; James 5: 16) and for all men including those in Government (1Tim. 2: 2). "Prayer of this kind is good, and God our saviour is pleased with it, for he wants all men to be saved and to come to know the truth" (1Tim. 2: 3-4).

PRAYER FOR THE POPE
O almighty and eternal God
Have mercy on ...N..., our Pope,
And direct him according to your clemency
Into the way of everlasting salvation;
That he may desire by your grace
Those things that are agreeable to you,
And perform them with all his strength.
Amen.

PRAYER FOR PRIESTS
Father, you have appointed
Your Son Jesus Christ,
Eternal High Priest:
Guide those he has chosen

To be ministers of word and sacrament
And help them to be faithful
In fulfilling the ministry they have received.
Grant this through our Lord Jesus Christ,
your Son,
Who lives and reigns with you and the Holy
Spirit,
One God forever and ever. Amen.

PRAYER FOR UNITY

O Lord Jesus Christ,
Who said to your apostles,
Peace I leave with you,
My peace I give to you;
Look not upon our sins,
But upon the faith of your Church
And grant to her that peace and unity
Which is according to your will;
Who live and reign forever and ever. Amen.

PRAYER FOR THE FAMILY

O Most Holy Trinity,
You are the perfect Family of all eternity.
Indivisible God,
In your perfect and one love,
Keep your children in this house

One family under your care.
Make us true to your name.
Let the light of Christ fill our home
That we may know and love one another
And share our every joy and sorrow
As we tread a path of peace and progress.
Make us rejoice in your blessings
And give us contentment.
Help us not to be distant from your cross
So that virtue may abound
And unite us in fruitfulness
In all affairs of our lives. Amen.

PRAYER OF THE GOOD SHEPHERD

Lord, make me a good shepherd
of your sheep,
A shepherd after your own heart.
In thought, in word, let me be deep,
Reflecting the rule of the Paraclete.
Guide me by your holy light,
You who are the truth and life;
Along with you to see and judge,
And rule with wisdom and love.
Let my word and deed be lesson,
To inspire good from every person,
Along a path of peace and patience,

Promoting freedom, respecting conscience,
Teach me to call each one a friend,
To risk my life and theirs defend.
Make it my joy to see them prosper,
And grow in joy and holiness.
And then in turn, from each to learn:
O Master – teach me lowliness.
Lord, with such compassion and true
affection,
You are the shepherd *par excellence:*
"I know my sheep and my own know me"
Open my eyes that I may see
All that is theirs; and add to my cares,
The need to sanctify these affairs.
With constant courage, keep me watchful.
In every combat, keep me lawful.
And by the power of your grace,
Each day's cross, make me embrace.
Lord, keep me serving constantly,
That they may have life – abundantly.

PRAYER FOR PEACE
Give peace, O Lord, in our days, for there is
no other to fight for us, but only you, our
God. May peace be ours through your
protection, O Lord, and prosperity through

your strong defense. O God, from whom are holy desires, right counsels and just deeds, give to your servants that peace which the world cannot give that we may serve you, with our whole hearts, and live quiet lives under your protection, free from the fear of our enemies, through Christ Our Lord. Amen.

PRAYER BEFORE WORK OR MEETINGS

Direct, we beg you, O Lord, our actions
By your inspirations,
And carry them on
By your gracious assistance,
That every prayer and work of ours
May begin always with you,
And through you be happily ended. Amen.

 # PENITENTIAL PRAYERS

PRAYERS BEFORE SACRAMENTAL CONFESSION

MISERERE (PSALM 51)
Have mercy on me, God, in your kindness.
In your compassion blot out my offence.
O wash me more and more from my guilt
And cleanse me from my sin.
My offences, truly I know them.
My sin is always before me.
Against you, you alone have I sinned;
What is evil in your sight I have done.
That you may be justified
When you give sentence
And be without reproach when you judge.
O see, in guilt I was born,
A sinner was I conceived.
Indeed you love truth in the heart.
Then in the secret of my heart
Teach me wisdom.
O purify me, then I shall be clean.
O wash me, I shall be whiter than snow.
Make me hear rejoicing and gladness,

That the bones you have crushed may thrill.
From my sins turn away your face,
And blot out all my guilt.
A pure heart create for me O God,
Put a steadfast spirit within me.
Do not cast me away from your presence,
Nor deprive me of your Holy Spirit.
Give me again the joy of your help,
With a spirit of fervor sustain me,
That I may teach transgressors your ways
And sinners may return to you.
O rescue me God my helper, and
My tongue shall ring out your goodness.
O Lord, open my lips
And my mouth shall declare your praise.
For in sacrifice you take no delight;
Burnt offering from me you would refuse.
My sacrifice - a contrite spirit;
A humbled contrite heart you will not spurn.
In your goodness, show favor to Zion:
Rebuild the walls of Jerusalem.
Then you will be pleased
With lawful sacrifice,
(Burnt offerings wholly consumed);
Then you will be offered
Young bulls on your altar. Amen.

PSALM 38
O Lord, in your anger punish me not,
In your wrath chastise me not;
For your arrows have sunk deep in me,
And your hand has come down upon me.
There is no health in my flesh
Because of your indignation;
There is no wholeness in my bones
Because of my sin,
For my iniquities have overwhelmed me;
They are like a heavy burden,
Beyond my strength.
Indeed, I acknowledge my guilt;
I grieve over my sin.
Forsake me not, O Lord;
My God, be not far from me!
Make haste to help me,
O Lord my salvation. Amen.

PRAYERS FOR AFTER SACRAMENTAL CONFESSION

PSALM 30 (abridged)
O Lord, my God,
I cried out to you and you healed me.
O Lord you brought me up

From the netherworld;
You preserved me from among those
Going down into the pit.
Sing praise to the Lord,
You his faithful ones,
And give thanks to his holy name.
For his anger lasts but a moment;
A lifetime his goodwill.
At nightfall weeping enters in,
But with the dawn, rejoicing.
You changed my mourning into dancing;
You took off my sackcloth
And clothed me with gladness,
That my soul might sing praise
To you without ceasing;
O Lord, my God,
Forever will I give you thanks. Amen.

PSALM 32
Happy is he whose fault is taken away,
Whose sin is covered.
Happy the man to whom
The Lord imputes no guilt,
In whose spirit there is no guile.
As long as I would not speak,
My bones wasted away

With my groaning all day,
For day and night
Your hand was heavy upon me;
My strength was dried up
As by the heat of summer.
Then I acknowledged my sin to you,
My guilt I covered not.
I said. "I confess my faults to the Lord,"
And you took away the guilt of my sin.
For this shall every faithful man
Pray to you in time of stress.
Though deep waters overflow,
They shall not reach him.
You are my shelter;
From distress you will preserve me;
With glad cries of freedom
You will ring me round. Amen.

PSALM 103
Bless the Lord, O my soul;
And all my being bless his holy name.
Bless the Lord, O my soul,
And forget not all his benefits;
He pardons all your iniquities,
He heals all your ills.
He redeems your life from destruction,

He crowns you
With kindness and compassion,
He fills your lifetime with good;
Your youth is renewed like the eagle's.
Merciful and gracious is the Lord,
Slow to anger and abounding in kindness.
He will not always chide,
Nor does he keep his wrath forever.
Nor according to our sins
Does he deal with us,
Nor does he requite us according
To our crimes.
For as the heavens are high above the earth,
So surpassing is his kindness
Toward those who fear him.
As far as the east is from the west,
So far has he put our transgressions from us.
As a father has compassion on his children,
So the Lord has compassion
On those who fear him,
For he knows how we are formed;
He remembers that we are dust.
Bless the Lord, all you his angels,
You mighty in strength, who do his bidding,
Obeying his spoken word.
Bless the Lord, all you his hosts,

His ministers who do his will.
Bless the Lord, all his works,
Everywhere in his domain.
Bless the Lord, O my soul! Amen.

PSALM 106
Give thanks to the Lord, for he is good,
For his kindness endures forever.
Who can tell the mighty deeds of the Lord,
Or proclaim all his praises?
Happy are they, who observe what is right,
Who do always what is just.
Remember me, O Lord,
As you favor your people;
Visit me with your saving help,
That I may see the posterity
Of your chosen ones,
Rejoice in the joy of your people,
And glory with your inheritance. Amen.

PSALM 116
I love the Lord because he has heard
My voice in supplication,
Because he has inclined his ear
To me the day I called.
The cord of death encompasses me;

The snares of the nether world
Seized upon me;
I fell into distress and sorrow,
And I called upon the name of the Lord,
"O Lord, save my life!"
Gracious is the Lord and just;
Yes, our God is merciful.
The Lord keeps the little ones;
I was brought low and he saved me.
Return, O my soul, to your tranquillity,
For the lord has been good to you.
For he has freed my soul from death,
My eyes from tears,
My feet from stumbling.
I shall walk before the Lord
In the lands of the living.
How shall I make a return to the Lord
For all the good he has done for me?
The cup of salvation I will take up,
And I will call upon the name of the Lord;
To you will I offer
Sacrifices of thanksgiving,
And I will call upon the name of the Lord.
Amen.

COMMUNION PRAYERS

This section is short because the period of physical and spiritual communion with Jesus in the Blessed Sacrament should be as spontaneous as possible to make it a personal encounter with Christ, the Bread of Life. "Is not the cup of blessing we bless a sharing in the blood of Christ? And is not the bread we break a sharing in the body of Christ?" (1Cor. 10: 16). "Every time, then, you eat this bread and drink this cup, you proclaim the death of the Lord until he comes! This means that whoever eats the bread or drinks the cup of the Lord unworthily sins against the body and blood of the Lord.... He who eats and drinks without recognising the body eats and drinks a judgement on himself" (1Cor. 11: 26-27,29). We should therefore take great care of our piety at Holy Communion. Where an aid is required, the following prayers or the sections of this book "To Know Jesus Christ" and "Aspirations" may be useful.

A PRAYER FOR HOLY COMMUNION
Come LORD JESUS,
Come into my heart
And espy its emptiness.
Speak to the FATHER

And send forth the SPIRIT
To make me a temple
Of your Pure Love.
Come Lord Jesus,
You are the Way,
The Truth and the Life,
My Alpha and Omega.
Show me the FATHER
For you are our Advocate.
O LOVING FATHER
God our Creator,
Look on our lowliness,
Here in this exile;
Recreate in us
The image of your Son,
Our Priest,
Our Altar,
Our Sacrifice. Amen.

A POST COMMUNION PRAYER
Come, Eternal High Priest
Sanctify my soul
Cleanse me Lord, with
Your Precious Blood and
Endless Holocaust.
Strengthen my being

O Bread of Life.
Recreate in me
Your Spirit Lord.
Make my heart like unto thine.
Come, O King of Kings
Lord Divine, I adore you.
To you I submit my all;
That you claim me,
And you rule me,
And use me as you will.
To you be thanks
And endless praise.
Come, O Word Incarnate
Teach me your Law.
Prophet of all prophets,
Engrave your law in me.
In the secret of my heart,
Teach me Wisdom
And I will announce
Your decree O Lord! Amen.

ADOROTE DEVOTE (St. Thomas Aquinas)
Hidden here before me,
   Lord I worship you.
   Hidden in these symbols,
   Yet completely true.

Lord, my soul surrenders,
Longing to obey,
And in contemplation
Wholly faints away.
Seeing, touching, tasting:
These are all deceived;
Only through the hearing
Can it be believed.
Nothing is more certain:
Christ has told me so;
What the truth has uttered,
I believe and know.
Only God was hidden
When you came to die:
Human nature also
Here escapes the eye.
Both are my profession,
Both are my belief:
Bring me to your Kingdom,
Like the dying thief.
I am not like Thomas,
Who would see and touch;
Though your wounds are hidden,
I believe as much.
Let me say so boldly,
Meaning what I say,

Loving you and trusting,
Now and every day.
Record of the passion
    When the lamb was slain,
    Living bread that brings us
    Back to life again:
    Feed me with your presence,
    Make me live on you;
    Let that lovely fragrance
    Fill me through and through.
Once a nesting pelican
    Gashed herself to blood
    For the preservation
    Of her starving brood;
    Now heal me with your blood,
    Take away my guilt:
    All the world is ransomed
    If one drop is spilt.
Jesus, for the present seen
    As through a mask,
    Give me what I thirst for,
    Give me what I ask:
    Let me see your glory
    In a blaze of light,
    And instead of blindness
    Give me, Lord, my sight. Amen.

JESUS HELP ME
In every need let me come to you
With humble trust saying,
Jesus, help me.
In all my doubts, temptations
And troubles of mind,
Jesus, help me.
When I am lonely or tired,
Jesus, help me.
When my plans and hopes have failed;
In all my disappointments and sorrows,
Jesus, help me.
When others let me down and
Your grace alone can assist me,
Jesus, help me.
When my heart is heavy with failure and
When I see no good come from my efforts,
Jesus, help me.
When I feel impatient, and
When my cross is hard to carry,
Jesus, help me.
When I am ill,
And my head and hands cannot work,
Jesus, help me.
Always, always, in spite of weakness
And falls of every kind,

Jesus, help me and never leave me. Amen.

ASPIRATIONS TO THE SACRED HEART

Most sacred and merciful Heart of Jesus,
>   Give us peace.

Sacred Heart of Jesus,
>   Thy Kingdom come.

Sacred Heart of Jesus,
>   I believe in your love for me.

Sacred Heart of Jesus,
>   I place my trust in you.

Sacred Heart of Jesus,
>   Make my heart like unto thine.

PETITIONS TO JESUS

Jesus, Son of the Eternal Father, convert me.
Jesus, Son of Mary, take me as her child.
Jesus, my Master, teach me.
Jesus, Prince of Peace, give me peace.
Jesus, my refuge, receive me.
Jesus, my Shepherd, feed my soul.
Jesus, model of patience, comfort me.
Jesus, meek and humble of heart,
Make me like you.
Jesus, my Redeemer, save me.
Jesus, my God and my All, possess me.
Jesus, the True Way, guide me.

Jesus, Eternal Truth, teach me.
Jesus, Life of the saints,
Make me live in you.
Jesus, my support, give me strength.
Jesus, my justice, make me good.
Jesus, Healer of my soul, heal me.
Jesus, my Judge, pardon me.
Jesus, my King, rule me.
Jesus, my holiness, make me holy.
Jesus, infinite goodness, pardon me.
Jesus, Living Bread from Heaven,
Be the food of my soul.
Jesus, my helper, help me.
Jesus, magnet of love, draw me.
Jesus, my protector, defend me.
Jesus, my hope, support me.
Jesus, object of love, unite me to yourself.
Jesus, fountain of Life, refresh me.
Jesus my Divine Victim, atone for me.
Jesus, my last end, let me possess you.
Jesus, my glory, glorify me. Amen.

APOSTOLATE PRAYERS 

THE APOSTLE'S PRAYER
Not easy it is
  To know you Lord,
Less easy it is
  To follow you.
I will at least try to
  Show you Lord
That others may come
  To hallow you. 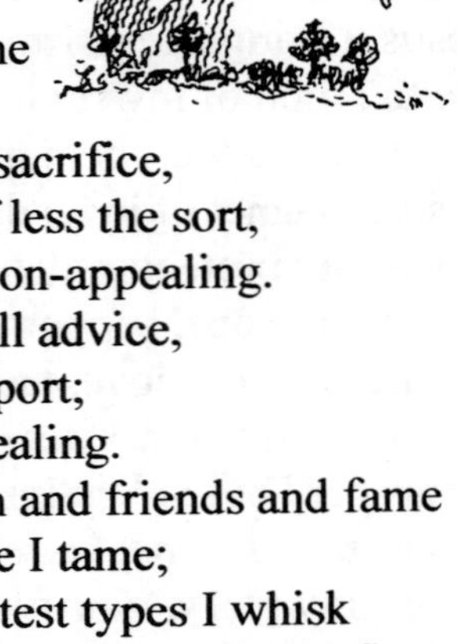
While people call it sacrifice,
I deem my choice of less the sort,
Though a madness non-appealing.
Against all good or ill advice,
I seek not men's support;
This way is non-repealing.
So health and wealth and friends and fame
I gain and lose as life I tame;
And dreams of sweetest types I whisk
For on your Beauty, God, my gaze to fix.
Amen.

PRAYER FOR SELF SURRENDER
Take from me, Lord,
All that takes me from you.
Give me, Lord,
All that leads to you.
Detach me, Lord, from myself
That I may give my all to you. Amen.

PRAYER FOR HUMILITY
Take from me, Lord,
  All pride and vanity;
  All boasting and forwardness,
And give me
  The true *courage* that
Shows itself in gentleness;
  The true *wisdom* that
Shows itself in simplicity and
  The true *power* that
Shows itself in humility. Amen.

PRAYER FOR A CLEAN HEART
Lord,
Make my heart more like thine
That I may see in others:
Their problems more than their faults,
Their struggles more than their weakness,

Their victories more than their failures,
Their sorrows more than their joys,
Their needs more than their wealth.
Lord,
Make me meek and humble of heart. Amen.

PRAYER FOR HOLY PURITY

Lord, give me holy purity,
The humility of the heart and flesh.
Give me wisdom to know
The perfect object of love
And light to place all things
In their order of beauty
And in their order in time
So that the first shall be first
And the last shall be last.
And give me courage Lord,
That what may not be will not be
And all that should be will be
And life will be a harmony
Within me and in all those you place by me.
Amen.

PRAYER FOR GENEROUSITY
Dearest Jesus, teach me to be generous.
Teach me to serve you as you deserve:
To give and not to count the cost;
To fight and not to heed the wounds;
To work and look for no reward
Except that of knowing
That I am doing your will. Amen.

PRAYER OF ST. AUGUSTINE
Lord Jesus,
May I know myself and know you
And desire nothing except you.
May I hate myself and love you
And do everything for your sake.
May I humble myself and exult you
And think of nothing except you.
May I die to myself and live in you.
May I receive whatever happens
As from you.
May I banish self and follow you
And ever desire to follow you.
May I fly from myself and fly to you
That I may deserve to be defended by you.
May I fear for myself and fear you
And be among those who are chosen by you.

May I distrust myself and trust you.
May I be willing to obey on account of you.
May I cling to nothing but you.
May I be poor for the sake of you.
Look upon me that I may love you.
Call me that I may see you
And ever and ever enjoy you. Amen.

PRAYER OF SAINT FRANCIS OF ASSISI
Lord,
Make me an instrument of Your peace.
Where there is hatred, let me sow love;
Where there is injury, let me sow pardon;
Where there is doubt, let me sow faith;
Where there is despair, let me sow hope;
Where there is darkness, let me sow light;
Where there is sadness, let me sow joy.
O Divine Master!
Grant that I may not so much seek
To be consoled as to console,
To be understood as to understand,
To be loved as to love: for,
It is in giving that we receive,
It is in pardoning that we are pardoned
It is in dying that we are born
To Eternal Life. Amen.

ST. PATRICK'S BREASTPLATE

I rise up today,
The power of God directing me,
The strength of God supporting me,
The wisdom of God guiding me,
The eye of God looking before me,
The ear of God listening to me,
The hand of God protecting me,
The way of God stretching out before me,
The shield of God defending me,
The angels of God guarding me,
Against snares of devils,
Against temptations and vices,
Against inclinations of nature,
Against anyone who wishes evil to me,
Christ with me,
Christ before me,
Christ behind me,
Christ in me,
Christ beneath me,
Christ above me,
Christ on my right hand,
Christ on my left hand,
Christ where I sit,
Christ where I rise,
Christ in the heart

Of anyone who thinks of me,
Christ in the mouth
Of anyone who speaks of me,
Christ in every eye that sees me,
Christ in every ear that hears me. Amen.

PRAYER TO WORK FOR THE SALVATION OF MANKIND

Lord Jesus Christ, Son of the living God,
You took our flesh to dwell among us.
Help me to see people as you see them;
To know people as you know them;
To understand people as you understand;
To love people as you love them;
To think of people as you think of them;
To speak to people as you speak to them;
To be with people as you are with them;
To serve people as you serve them;
To hear people as you hear them;
To forgive people as you forgive.
Lord, Let me partake of
The work of salvation. Amen.

PRAYER FOR VOCATIONS

Lord Jesus Christ,
Shepherd of souls,
Who called the Apostles
To be fishers of men,
Raise up new apostles
In your Holy Church.
Teach them that
To serve you is to reign;
To possess you
Is to possess all things.
Kindle in the young hearts
Of our people
The fire of zeal for souls.
Make them eager
To spread your Kingdom
Upon earth.
Grant them courage
To follow you
Who are The Way
The Truth and
The Life.
Who lives and reigns forever and ever.
Amen.

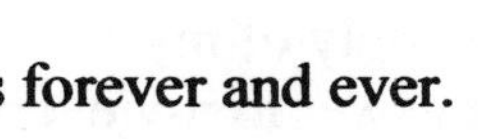

 # PRAYERS FOR GOD'S PROVIDENCE 

The most important prayer is the OUR FATHER which is included in the Popular Prayers. Jesus taught us to call God "Our Father" (Luke 11: 1-3) and the Holy Spirit enables us to do so in reality and effectively as adopted children (Romans 8: 14-16).

PRAYER FOR VIRTUOUS LIVING

O God my Loving Father,
May I always enjoy your fatherly care:
The Grace of your Holy Spirit;
The supernatural light and knowledge of
Your Son Jesus Christ;
The peace of good conscience;
The freedom and confidence of the just;
The consolation of your Holy Spirit;
And your sustenance in affliction.
May I enjoy always:
Your supply of my temporal needs;
Your answer to my every prayer;
Your favor in every respect,
And above all, in the name of Jesus,
The happy death of the just. Amen.

PRAYER OF THE CHILD OF GOD
Lord God, my Loving Father,
In the name of Christ I pray;
Make me more your child each day
Save me from the erroneous way.
Make me humble but never timid;
Make me simple but never stupid;
Make me truthful but never proud;
Make me diligent but never loud;
Make me patient but not a coward;
Make me courageous but not forward;
Make me chaste but never callous,
Make me pious but not too obvious.
Help me be human and divine with tact,
That I may think and speak and act
Like Christ, my Lord True God, True Man
And trace His steps as best I can. Amen.

PSALM 2
Why do the nations rage
And the peoples utter folly?
The kings of the earth rise up
And the princes conspire together
Against the Lord and against his anointed:
"Let us break their fetters
And cast their bonds from us!"

He who is 'throned in Heaven laughs;
The Lord derides them.
Then in anger he speaks to them;
He terrifies them in his wrath:
"I myself have set up my king
On Zion, my holy mountain."
I will proclaim the decree of the Lord:
The Lord said to me, "You are my son;
This day I have begotten you.
Ask of me and I will give you
The nations for an inheritance
And the ends of the earth
For your possession.
You shall rule them with an iron rod;
You shall scatter them like an earthen dish."
And now, O kings give heed;
Take warning, you rulers of the earth.
Serve the Lord with fear,
And rejoice before him;
With trembling pay homage to him,
Lest he be angry
And you perish from the way,
When his anger blazes suddenly.
Happy are all who take
Refuge in him! Amen.

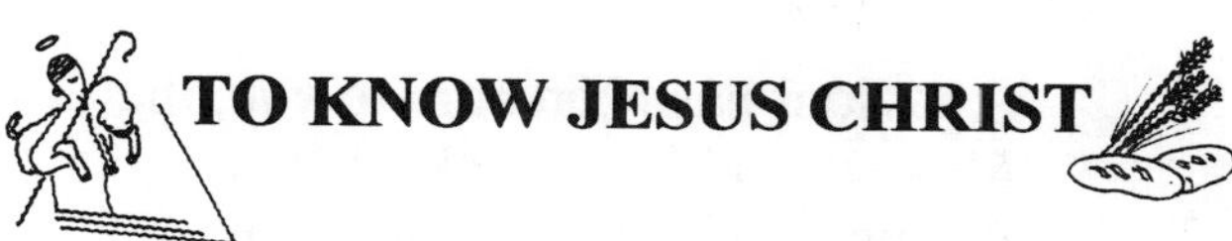

TO KNOW JESUS CHRIST

"Eternal life is this: to know you, the only true God, and him whom you have sent, Jesus Christ" (John 17: 3).

It is good to meditate on the New Testament because there we meet Jesus and get to know Him. St Peter warns us that to keep from error and to be secured, we must "..grow in grace and in the knowledge of Our Lord and Saviour Jesus Christ" (2Peter 3: 18). As we read the Gospel carefully, we will have facts about Him that cling to our memory and guide our thoughts and actions such as the ones below. We may find it useful to speak to Jesus about them and ask Him for graces for ourselves and for other people concerning these words especially in the intimacy with Him on receiving Holy Communion. In this way we too, like St. Paul, will enjoy above all other possessions and all gain " the supreme advantage of knowing Christ Jesus" (Phil 3: 8).

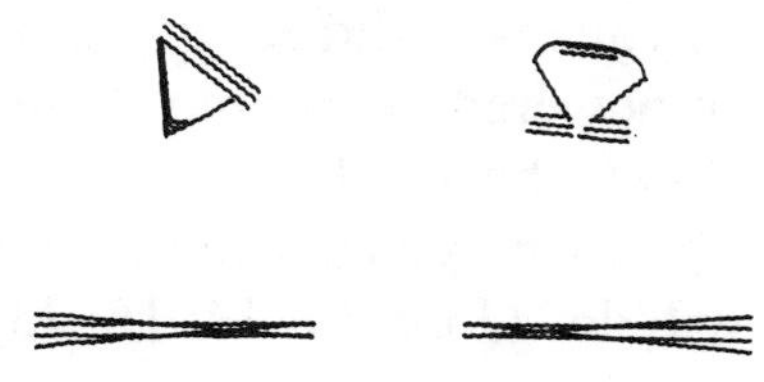

1. A saviour has been born to you, the Messiah and Lord (Luke 2: 11).

2. A voice came from the heavens: "You are my beloved Son. On you my favor rests" (Matt. 1: 11).

3. "Accursed be that man by whom the son of man is betrayed" (Mark 14: 21).

4. After his sufferings, he showed them in many convincing ways that he was alive (Acts 1: 3).

5. "All men will honor the Son just as they honor the Father" (John 5: 23).

6. All the disciples deserted Him and fled (Matt. 26: 56).

7. All who heard Him were amazed at His intelligence and answers (Luke 2: 47).

8. "Am I not to drink the cup the Father has given me?" (John 18: 11).

9. Anyone who did accept Him, he empowered to become children of God (John 1: 12).

10. "Anything you ask in my name, I will do" (John 14: 14; 16: 23).

11.   "Apart from me, you can do nothing" (John 15: 5).

12.   As he entered Jerusalem, the whole city was stirred to its depths (Matt. 21: 10).

13.   "As the Father has loved me, so I have loved you" (John 15: 9).

14.   At the Name of Jesus, every knee must bend (Phil. 2: 10).

15.   "Because of my name, you will be hated by everyone" (Mark 13: 13).

16.   Beyond doubt…the Son of God (Matt. 14: 33).

17.   Call Him Emanuel…God with us (Matt. 1: 23).

18.   "Can anyone convict me of sin?" (John 8: 46).

19.   Children were shouting "Hosanna to the Son of David" (Matt. 21: 15).

20.   Christ came to bring about our justification through faith (Gal. 3: 24).

21.   Christ is all things and in all (Col. 3: 11).

22.   Christ is the end of the Law (Romans 10: 4).

23.   "Come after me and I will make you
      fishers of men" (Matt. 4: 19).
24.   "Come to me all you who are weary
      and find life burdensome and I will
      refresh you" (Matt. 11: 28).
25.   "Did you not know that I had to be in
      my Father's house?" (Luke 2: 49;
      John 2: 17).
26.   Even the winds and the sea obey
      Him (Matt. 8: 27).
27.   "Everyone who looks upon the Son
      and believes in him shall have
      eternal life" (John 6: 40).
28.   For our sake, he made himself poor
      though he was rich (cf. 2Cor. 8: 9).
29.   "From the cup I drink of, you shall
      drink" (Matt. 20: 23).
30.   God has visited His people (Luke 7:
      16).
31.   God so loved the world that He gave
      his only Son (John 3: 16).
32.   He came walking towards them on
      the water (Mark 6: 48).
33.   He cured them all (Matt. 4: 24).

34.   He did not deem equality to God something to cling to but emptied himself (Philippians 2: 6-7).

35.   He fasted forty days and forty nights (Matt. 4: 2).

36.   He gave himself for us as an offering to God, a gift of pleasing fragrance (Eph. 5: 2).

37.   He gives orders to unclean spirits and they obey Him (Mark 1: 27).

38.   He has done all things well (Mark 7: 37).

39.   He interpreted for them every passage of the scriptures (Luke 24: 27).

40.   He is the image of the invisible God (Col. 1: 15).

41.   He knew their thoughts (Luke 6: 8).

42.   He knew what was in man (John 2: 24-25; Luke 6: 8).

43.   He loved me and sacrificed Himself for me (cf. Galatians 2: 20).

44.   He loved us to the end (cf. John 13: 1).

45.   He made the deaf to hear and the mute to speak (Mark 7: 37).

46.   He often retired to desert places and prayed (Luke 5: 16).

47.   He progressed steadily in wisdom and age and grace before God and men (Luke 2: 52).

48.   He sacrificed himself for us (Titus 2: 14).

49.   He taught with authority (Mark 1: 22).

50.   He was absorbed in prayer (Mark 1: 35).

51.   He was counted among the wicked (Isaiah 53: 12).

52.   He was in the world, and through him the world was made, yet the world did not know who he was (John 1: 10).

53.   He was known to be of human estate (Phil. 2: 7).

54.   He was obedient to them (his parents) (Luke 22: 51).

55.   He was transfigured before their eyes (Matt. 17: 2; Mark 9: 2).

56.   "He who brings himself to naught for me discovers who he is" (Matt. 10: 39).

57.   "He who does not gather with me scatters" (Matt. 12: 30).
58.   "He who eats my flesh and drinks my blood has eternal life" (John 6: 55).
59.   "He who is not with me is against me" (Matt. 12: 30).
60.   "He who lives in me and I in him will produce abundantly" (John 15: 5).
61.   "He who loves me will be loved by my Father" (John 15: 21).
62.   He will repay each man according to his conduct Matt. 16: 27).
63.   He wills that all men be saved and come to the knowledge of truth (1Tim. 2: 4).
64.   His offence read: "King of the Jews" (Mark 15: 26).
65.   "I am in your midst as one who serves" (Luke 22: 27).
66.   "I am indeed going to prepare a place for you" (John 14: 3).
67.   "I am the alpha and omega" (Rev. 1: 8; 21: 6).

68.   "I am the door of the sheepfold"
        (John 10: 9).
69.   "I am the Good Shepherd" (John 10:
        14, 27).
70.   "I am the light of the world" (John 8:
        12).
71.   "I am the Resurrection and the Life"
        (John 11: 25).
72.   "I am the vine, you are the branches"
        (John 15: 5).
73.   "I am the Way, the Truth and the
        Life" (John 10: 11).
74.   "I came into this world to divide it,
        to make the sightless see and the
        seeing blind" (John 9: 39).
75.   "I give you a new commandment:
        Love one another" (John 13: 34, 15:
        12, 15: 17).
76.   "I have called you friends" (John 15:
        15).
77.   "I have come to call not the self-
        righteous, but sinners" (Matt. 9: 13).
78.   "I have come to light a fire on earth"
        (Luke 12: 49).
79.   "I have overcome the world" (John
        16: 33).

80.   "I will make you fishers of men"
        (Matt. 4: 19; Mark 1: 17).
81.   "I will not leave you orphaned"
        (John 14: 18).
82.   "I, myself, am the bread of life"
        (John 6: 35, 48, 51).
83.   "I, once I am lifted up from the earth,
        will draw all men to myself" (John
        12: 32).
84.   "If a man wishes to come after me he
        must deny himself, take up his cross
        and begin to follow in my footsteps"
        (Matt. 16: 24; Mark 8: 34).
85.   If anyone is in Christ, he is a new
        creation (2Cor. 5: 17).
86.   "If anyone serves me, he the Father
        will honor" (John 12: 26).
87.   "If anyone thirsts, let him come to
        me and drink" (John 7: 37).
88.   "If I had not come to them and
        spoken to them, they would not be
        guilty of sin" (John 15: 22).
89.   "If the Son frees you, you will be
        free indeed" (John 8: 36).

90.   "If you live according to my teaching, you are truly my disciples" (John 8: 31).

91.   "If you really knew me you would know the Father also" (John 14: 7).

92.   In Christ Jesus, the Gentiles are now co-heirs with the Jews (Eph. 3: 6).

93.   In Him dwells all the fullness of the Godhead bodily (Col. 2: 9).

94.   In His Name, the gentiles will find hope (Matt. 12: 21).

95.   "In me you will find peace" (John 16: 33).

96.   In the beginning was the Word, the Word was God (John 1: 1).

97.   "In this is my Father glorified – that you bear much fruit" (John 15: 8).

98.   It was impossible that death should keep its hold on him (Acts 2: 24).

99.   "It was not you who chose me, it was I who chose you to go forth and bear fruit" (John 15: 16).

100.   It was our infirmities he bore, our sufferings he endured (Isaiah 53: 4; Matt. 8: 17).

101.　It was out of jealousy that they handed Him over (Matt. 27: 18).

102.　Jesus Christ is the same yesterday, today, and forever (Hebrews 13: 8).

103.　Jesus remained silent (Matt. 26: 63).

104.　Jesus rose from the dead (Mark 16: 9).

105.　Jesus wept (John 11: 35).

106.　Jesus, tired from his journey sat down at the well (John 4: 6).

107.　"Learn from me for I am meek and humble of heart" (Matt. 11: 29).

108.　Like a sheep led to the slaughter, he was silent and opened not his mouth (Isaiah 53: 7; cf. Acts 8: 32).

109.　Like us in all things but sin (Heb. 4: 14-16; 5: 7-9).

110.　"Live on in me as I live in you" (John 15: 4).

111.　"My grace is sufficient for you" (2Cor. 12: 9).

112.　"My heart is moved with pity for the crowd" (Matt. 15: 32).

113.　"My kingdom is not of this world" (John 18: 36).

114. "My meat is to do the will of he who sent me, to accomplish the task he gave me" (John 4: 34).
115. "My yoke is easy and my burden is light" (Matt. 11: 30).
116. Never did man speak like this man (John 7: 46).
117. "No follower of mine shall ever walk in darkness" (John 8: 12).
118. "No one comes to the Father but by me" (John 14: 6).
119. No one who believes in him will be put to shame (Romans 10: 11).
120. "None of you can be my disciple if he does not renounce his possessions" (Luke 14: 33).
121. Obedient unto death, death on a cross (Phil. 2: 8).
122. "Peace is my farewell to you, my peace is my gift to you" (John 14: 27).
123. "Such as my love has been for you, so must your love be for each other" (John 13: 34).
124. The carpenter, the son of Mary (Mark 6: 3).

125.   The crowds kept answering, "This is
        the prophet Jesus" (Matt. 21: 10).
126.   "The Father and I are one" (John 10:
        30).
127.   "The Father is in me and I in Him"
        (John 10: 38, 14: 11).
128.   The found the child with Mary his
        mother…(Matt. 2: 11).
129.   "The heavens and earth will pass
        away but my words will not pass
        away" (Matt. 24: 35).
130.   The King of kings, Lord of lords
        (Rev. 19: 16).
131.   The King of the Jews (Mark 15: 26;
        Luke 23: 38; John 19: 19).
132.   The Lamb of God who takes away
        the sin of the world (John 1: 29).
133.   The Light came into the world but
        men loved darkness rather than light
        (John 3: 19).
134.   The Lord Jesus was taken up into
        Heaven (Mark 16: 19).
135.   "The man who has faith in me will
        do the works I do and greater far
        than these" (John 14: 12).

136. The Messiah......the Son of the
      Living God (Matt. 16: 16).
137. The Son of God...King of Israel
      (John 1: 49).
138. The Son of man appeared eating and
      drinking (Matt. 11: 19).
139. "The Son of man has come to search
      out and save what was lost" (Luke
      19: 10).
140. "The Son of Man has nowhere to lay
      His head" (Luke 9: 58).
141. "The Son of Man will come with His
      Father's glory accompanied by His
      angels" (Matt. 16: 27).
142. "The Son of Man...has not come to
      be served...but to serve...and to give
      his life as a ransom for many" (Matt.
      20: 28).
143. The stone which the builders rejected
      became the keystone of the structure
      (Mark 12: 10; Luke 20: 17; Acts 4:
      11).
144. The whole crowd was under the spell
      of his teaching (Mark 11: 18; Luke
      4: 32).

145.   The Word became flesh and dwelt
       among us (John 1: 14).
146.   Their amazement of Him knew no
       bounds (Mark 12: 17).
147.   There is no salvation in anyone else
       (Acts 4: 12).
148.   They did not grasp what He said to
       them (Luke 2: 50).
149.   They found Him too much for them
       (Mark 6: 3).
150.   ''They hated me without cause''
       (John 12: 37, 15: 25).
151.   They refused to believe in me (John
       16: 9).
152.   They shall all be taught by God
       (John 6: 45).
153.   This child is destined to be the rise
       and fall of many in Israel (Luke 2:
       34).
154.   "This is everlasting life, that they
       may know the only true God and him
       whom thou has sent" (John 17: 3).
155.   "This is how all will know you for
       my disciples, by your love for one
       another" (John 13: 35).

156.   "This is the will of my Father, that anyone who looks upon the Son and believes in Him shall have Eternal Life" (John 6: 40).

157.   "This is the Work of God, have faith in the one whom He sent" (John 6: 29).

158.   "This, my father loves in me: that I lay down my life for my sheep" (John 10: 17).

159.   Through Him, all things came into being (John 1: 3).

160.   Took the form of a slave (Phil. 2: 7).

161.   Truly this man was the Son of God (Mark 15: 39).

162.   We are saved by the favor of the Lord Jesus (Acts 15: 11).

163.   We know that this really is the Savior of the world (John 4: 42).

164.   When he suffered, he threatened not (1 Peter 2: 23).

165.   "Where two or three are gathered in my name, there I am in their midst" (Matt. 18: 20).

166.   "Whoever does the will of my Heavenly Father is brother, sister and mother to me" (Matt. 12: 5).

167.   "Whoever drinks the water I give him will never be thirsty" (John 4: 14).

168.   "Whoever welcomes one such child for my sake welcomes me" (Matt. 18: 5).

169.   "Why do you call me 'Lord, Lord' and do not put into practice what I teach you?" (Luke 6: 46).

170.   "Without me you can do nothing" (John 15: 5).

171.   Word of God (Rev. 19: 13).

172.   "You address me as 'Teacher' and 'Lord'… for that is what I am" (John 13: 13).

173.   "You are my friends if you do what I command you" (John 15: 14).

174.   "You did not choose me. I chose you" (John 15: 16).

175.   "You have a greater than Jonah here…You have a greater than Solomon here" (Matt. 12: 41-42).

176.   "You will surely die in your sins unless you come to believe that I AM" (John 8: 24).

177.   "Your fruit must endure so that all you ask the Father in my name, He will give you" (John 15: 16).

THE BEATITUDES

(Jesus' Great Sermon in Matt. 5: 3-11; Luke 6: 20-23). It is in the beatitudes that the Cross of Christ finds its true expression in Christian life.

Blessed are the poor in spirit;
Theirs is the Kingdom of Heaven.
Blessed are they that mourn;
For they shall be comforted.
Blessed are they that
Hunger and thirst after justice;
For they shall have their fill.
Blessed are the merciful;
For they shall obtain mercy.
Blessed are the clean of heart;
For they shall see God.
Blessed are the peacemakers;
For they shall be called
The children of God.
Blessed are they that suffer
Persecution for justice' sake;
For theirs is the Kingdom of Heaven.
Blessed are the meek;
For they shall possess the land.

- *Those who are poor in spirit are content, generous, detached, and do not envy. They have a view of their last end - Heaven.*
- *Those who mourn are contrite, mortified, make sacrifices, resign to the will of God and do not despair. They see God's doing in everything.*
- *Those who seek justice love truth, and conscience, and spare the world of hatred. Their labor is always fruitful.*
- *Those who are merciful are understanding and loveable and have true self-knowledge before God and men.*
- *Those who are clean of heart have goodwill, sound judgement, and harmony and pray with ease.*
- *Those who are peacemakers promote unity and progress and reflect the dignity of man.*
- *Those who suffer persecution are neither ashamed of God nor afraid of men and have easy access to the blessings of God.*
- *Those who are meek are easy companions and are trusted by their fellow men.*

LITANY TO JESUS CHRIST

Lord, have mercy on us
Christ, have mercy on us
Lord, have mercy
Jesus, hear us
Jesus, graciously hear us

God the Father of Heaven	Have mercy on us
God, the Son the Redeemer of the world	"
God, the Holy Ghost	"
Holy Trinity, one God	"
Jesus, Son of the Living God	"
Jesus, glory of the Father	"
Jesus, brightness of Eternal Life	"
Jesus, King of Heaven	"
Jesus, shining with holiness	"
Jesus, son of the Virgin Mary	"
Jesus, most loveable	"
Jesus, most admirable	"
Jesus, all powerful God	"
Jesus, having loving care for our future	"
Jesus, bringing great news	"
Jesus, most powerful	"
Jesus, most patient	"
Jesus, most obedient	"
Jesus, most meek and humble of heart	"
Jesus, lover of chastity	"
Jesus, lover of us	"
Jesus, God of peace	"
Jesus, author of life	"
Jesus, model of virtues	"
Jesus, zealous for souls	"
Jesus, our God	"
Jesus, our protector	"
Jesus, lover of poor	"
Jesus, treasure of the faithful	"
Jesus, Good Shepherd	"
Jesus, true light of our souls	"
Jesus, eternal wisdom	"
Jesus, infinite Goodness	"
Jesus, our way and our life	"
Jesus, joy of angels	"

Jesus, King of patriarchs	"
Jesus, Master of apostles	"
Jesus, teacher of evangelists	"
Jesus, light of confessors	"
Jesus, purity of virgins	"
Jesus, reward of all the saints	"
Be merciful, spare us, O Jesus	"
Be merciful, graciously hear us, O Jesus	"
From all evil	O Jesus deliver us
From all sin	"
From your anger	"
From the snares of the devil	"
From the spirit of impurity	"
From everlasting death	"
From the neglect of your grace	"
Through your holy incarnation	"
Through your nativity	"
Through your infancy	"
Through your most divine life	"
Through your labours	"
Through your agony and passion	"
Through your cross and loneliness	"
Through your weakness	"
Through your death and burial	"
Through your resurrection	"
Through your joys	"
Through your glory	"
Lamb of God, you take away the sins of the world	Spare us, O Jesus
Lamb of God, you take away the sins of the world	Graciously hear us , O Jesus
Lamb of God, You take away the sins of the world	Have mercy on us, O Jesus

LET US PRAY:

O Lord Jesus Christ, who said: Ask and you shall receive; seek, you shall find; knock and it will be opened to you, grant to us who ask, the gift of your most divine love, that with all our heart, words and works, we may love you, and never cease to praise you.

Give us, O Lord, a perpetual fear and love of your Holy Name, for you never cease to guide those whom you firmly establish in your love. Amen.

THE STATIONS OF THE CROSS

All creatures feel pain, loss, want etc. Human beings experience suffering which involves the intellect. Suffering touches and alters every human life from birth to death. Whatever our conditions or status in life and even if we enjoy the "good things of this life" in abundance - money, honours, fame, wealth, fun, friends, power – we meet suffering everyday. Though it is a consequence of evil, Omnipotent God uses it to lead people unto good or to deter them from further evil. "He chastens us to keep us from being condemned" (1Cor. 11: 32). We meet suffering in different ways and for different reasons. Our suffering may be a product of sin, omission, inheritance or choice. A person can choose suffering by his intellect and will. A person can also love suffering by the motion of his heart.

There are two types of suffering: those that dignify man and raise him above his fallen nature making him graceful and those that disgrace man and reflect his fallen nature. As a Christian journeys through life, with God as his Father, he experiences transformation, through grace, from the fallen nature to the redeemed nature won for him by Jesus Christ. This experience encompasses different sufferings: punishment, natural suffering, moral suffering, environmental suffering, until he remains with the sufferings proper of Christians - the beatitudes.

Punishment *is an immediate consequence of deliberate personal sin. It comes in different forms such as physical pain, moral shame, social dishonor, disturbance of conscience and loss of grace. St. Paul gives us an example in 1Cor. 11: 30 – "That is why many among you are sick and infirm, and why so many are dying". St. Peter also refers to suffering that comes from sin (1Peter 4: 15). Such suffering involves a loss of dignity, but the experience of it weakens the power of malice for it deters people from future sin and opens the way to conversion. Punishment is not proper in correct Christian living: "Non of you should ever deserve to suffer for being a murderer, a thief, a criminal or an informer" (1Peter 4: 13-16).*

Natural suffering *is derived from mankind's inherited fallen nature; from the provisions or limitations of our flesh and intellect. God made the world good. Sin brought disorder, imperfection, danger and pain into the world. The human body is thus provided with the means to detect danger through suffering. Such suffering comes through hunger, thirst, pain, tiredness, fear, anxiety, as well as emotional and psychological distress. Jesus, having taken the nature of mankind, shared in this kind of suffering and thus we are assured it is sanctified and can sanctify. When it is good for us to face such suffering or when they cannot be avoided, God's grace helps us to do so with dignity as Jesus did in* *his temptation in the desert, his persecution by the Jewish authorities, and his agony in the garden. Many natural sufferings come to us as passive experiences but we also have the power to freely impose such suffering on ourselves actively as in fasting and abstinence.*

*   **Moral suffering** is imposed on each person by his or her condition as a social creature sharing life with other people equally prone to ignorance, disobedience, error and sin. Such suffering has its root in sin, especially the seven capital sins - pride, covetousness, lust, anger, gluttony, envy and sloth. These sins disturb the comfort of human society producing conditions such as confusion, rivalry, oppression, injustice, exploitation, disorder and war. The consequence is collective suffering. Such suffering is a dictate of malice turning people against each other to destroy human family. The guilty subjects or active participants suffer uselessly while the victim objects or passive participants may also suffer uselessly or may experience purification with dignity according to the employment of available grace. Moral suffering is common to Christians and Non-Christians alike. It is the duty of all to pray against such suffering at individual or social levels.*

*   **Environmental suffering** derives from each person's time and place in life and on the level of mankind's dominion over creation in such circumstance. God made the world and saw it was good and gave mankind authority to subdue the earth and*

to have dominion over other living things (Gen. 1: 28-31).   The inability to possess such integrity is associated with mankind's inherited fallen nature and distance from God. Ignorance, sickness, disability, want and catastrophes abound where we lack the virtue to overcome them. Natural disasters such as earthquakes, famine, plagues; supernatural disasters such as diabolic possessions and mysteries; and man-made disasters such as frustrations and accidents will be with us till the end of time because of mankind's determined distance from God and the need for us to be reminded of it. Day by day, we advance scientifically, technologically and culturally and civilisation is heightened. Mankind's dominion over creation is however not the original light and pleasure and entails effort, suffering and limitation but these are always fruitful and advance the common good. Jesus worked as a carpenter in His hidden life teaching us to strive for our livelihood and dignity. In His public life, He always relieved the punishment and undignifying sufferings that people had from the first miracle of providing wine at Cana to the feeding of the thousands, cure of ailments, calming of the storm and raising of the dead. Jesus always desired and cared for the physical and, above all, spiritual integrity of each person.   Likewise, the alleviation of degrading sufferings in a society is a mark of civilisation - the dominion of mankind over his environment. Without environmental suffering, this innate gift of dominion that mankind has would lack stimulus and would be a sterile and unfulfilled potency.   God continues to bless all humans, letting his sun and his rain to fall on the good and bad alike, respecting the intended status of all men and women as masters over his creation. God readily allows people to enjoy the temporal goods of this earth when they strive for it. However to have the pleasure of eternal life with Him is a duty of each person to earn of his or her own accord (if possible) or through our advocate Jesus Christ.

*   **The Beatitudes** are the sufferings proper of saints. Saints are men and women who have prepared themselves to be with God for all eternity by acquiring Charity. Suffering for no purpose is not Christian and is even foolish. The beatitudes are dictates of Charity on earth. These sufferings are a result of acceptance of grace, resolve, struggle and obedience to God's law. They are the sufferings encountered through practice of virtue, restraint from sin, submission to truth and sacrifice. They are above our natural tendencies but are within our nature to experience. They require the exercise of the free will of each person - that is, we participate actively. They are necessary for being Christian and are accommodated by the aid of Sacramental Grace. Through the Beatitudes, we are identified with the Cross of Christ ("...from the cup I drink of, you shall drink" (Matt. 20: 23)) and his imperative command for us to take up our cross daily and follow him (Matt. 16: 24; Mark 8: 34). It has nothing to do with fatalism, sadism, cynicism or weakness because, "greater is He who is in you than he who is in the*

world" (1John 4: 4). Indeed the devil is restless in this world (1Peter 5:8; Rev. 12: 12) and continues to operate under defeat. For this reason, "...the brotherhood of believers is undergoing the same sufferings throughout the world" (1Peter 5:9). Christian suffering is encountered through sacrifice made by Christian love unto the achievement of eternal good. The essence is not so much to pay off the debts from our sins (Christ did that, 1Tim. 2:5-6) but to participate in the work of salvation, contributing that little that corresponds to us, the portion of love that is ours to give (cf. Acts 9:16; 21:13). Such sacrifice is actualized in practice of virtue, correction of error, service and accomplishment of good work, and acts of generosity and mercy to fellow men and women, within a hostile environment of the Devil's rage.

However, before sacrifice, the most necessary pain and the most gainful is the pain of restraint - resisting evil within oneself (Hebrews 12:4) - denying the fallen nature to allow the Christian life of grace to increase within us: "..he who loses his life for my sake, will find it" (Matt. 10: 39). It takes a lot to deny the self that seeks exaltation, that seeks vengeance, that hates humiliation, that tends to the capital sins or any sin. It is even more suffering to refrain from weakness, frailties and imperfections because the line of least resistance appears to be more comfortable. However, we must undergo the "discipline of sons" (Hebrews 12: 7). If we allow ourselves to be justified we will fully enjoy the glory of the born-again: divine filiation, the life of grace, the life of God, the power of God, the power of love, the power of wisdom, of mercy, of magnanimity, the likeness of Christ, the Christian. We remain the particular individuals we are but blessed and happy, having transformed from the likeness of the earthy, to bear the likeness of the heavenly (1Cor. 15: 49).

The "eye for an eye and tooth for a tooth" which on a human level would be just enough underrates a Christian who has so much power of grace. We are empowered to absorb persecution, insults, misunderstanding, rash judgement, false accusation, calumny, consequences of our weakness and incapacities, disappointments, loss, and failure (2Cor. 4: 8-10; 2Cor. 6: 4-10). We are empowered to overcome the fallen nature and to restrain ourselves from thoughts, words and deeds that are inappropriate to our Christian vocation and mission in life. St. Paul in good faith boasts of his sufferings in the light of his gains (2Cor. 11: 23 – 33, 12: 7). As he saw clearly: against the evil in the world, man is glorified through suffering. "As for me, God forbid that I should glory save in the cross of Our Lord Jesus Christ, through whom the world is crucified to me, and I to the world" (Galatians 6: 14).

When we experience the Beatitudes, we tend to relieve fellow men and women from sin, ignorance, and the other types of sufferings that are not beatitudes, to annul the effect of sin in the world and to raise our work to God's work. Such suffering makes us one with Christ who bore the sin of the world. Our lives would contribute to sanctifying the world and building up a just society. Saint Peter says, "If it is God's will that you suffer, it is better to do so for good deeds than for evil ones" (1Peter 3: 17). Through such suffering, we identify closely with Jesus as Children of God and heirs of His glory (Romans 8: 17). Therefore it is in such suffering we rejoice: "Rejoice in the measure that you share Christ's sufferings" (1Peter 4: 13).

The Way of the cross is the only correct Christian path: "Enter through the narrow gate. The gate that leads to damnation is wide, the road is clear and many choose to travel it. But how narrow is the gate that leads to life, how rough the road, and how few there are who find it!" (Matt. 13: 14).

We need to find ways of growing in the awareness of the importance of suffering. It is good that we frequently reflect on the sufferings of Our Lord and unite our own sufferings to his infinite merit. Catholics have traditionally prayed with the Stations of the Cross on Fridays and during Lent and it is a very enriching custom. Here are a few points to help our Friday reflections but we should remember that the Holy Spirit is ready to give each person independent inspirations and we may learn totally different lessons from each station in our personal meditations. There are beautiful stations in the Parishes and it is good to remind people of the devotions to the Way of the Cross by using those inspiring stations ourselves.

First station. Jesus is condemned to death.
To many people, even Christians, it does not matter that we continue to condemn him to death. Some people may smugly abandon Christianity as old fashioned, a thing of the past. Many modern people have decided not to need God. When people drop God they will replace him with something else and idolatry will abound: how we exalt money, sex, fun, fame, or worst still – self, for the human soul was made to love God and "our hearts are restless till they rest in Him" (St. Augustine of Hippo). God's grace will help us to do what is effective to bring people back to Him.

Second station.   Jesus takes up his cross.

It is mysterious that God should want to redeem the world by taking up human nature to dwell among us and to suffer the shameful punishment of the cross.   It is mysterious that there is no day in our lives that we do not meet suffering. It is a wonder that we do not reflect much on the value of suffering and the way of the cross opened up to us, sanctified for us, glorified for us, and made fertile for us by the Son of God Almighty.   Acceptance of this way is a source of peace in our lives.

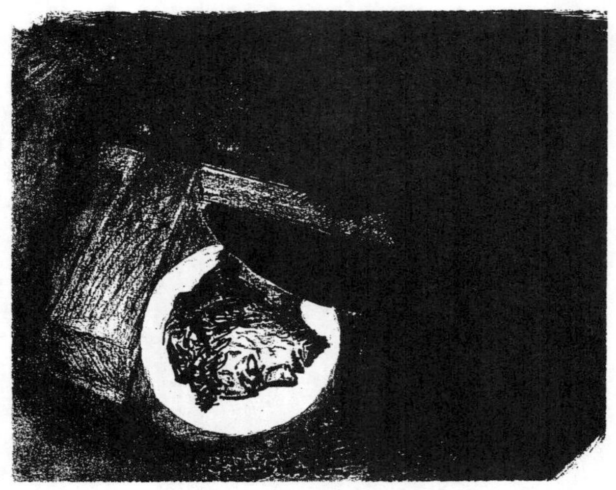

Third station. Jesus falls the first time.

The cross of Jesus: our sins, the consequences of sins, weigh so much. We too feel a bit of that weight. We must not despair. How often people turn to drugs, drink, fun, murder, suicide - trying to avoid further suffering! If only we would keep to the way of the cross, get up, carry it, continue to the end, safely, where glory awaits us, how little will be the suffering we would meet on the way. May God make us truly wise.

Fourth station. Jesus is met by His Blessed Mother.

When we walk with Christ we too will discover we are not alone. We would gladly go the way of the cross for there we meet many good people: Mary, our Blessed Mother cares and we have the whole communion of saints and our guardian angels at our disposal. Jesus has made this way the most pleasant for men on earth and so full of holy consolations. We should thank God for the communion of Saints.

Fifth station. Simon of Cyrene helps Jesus to carry the cross.

God is patient. God is merciful. But God is also just. Sin must be punished. Jesus has redeemed us from the punishment we deserve. Do people know it? Do people care? Do people want Jesus? Do people want redemption? No, not 'advanced' people. And so we need Simons of Cyrene who would carry the cross and make the way of redemption known to their companions. We ourselves first, will freely and generously help with the work of salvation.

Sixth station. The face of Jesus is wiped by Veronica.

The human being has become his own god. What an insult to the true God. What an insult to the Incarnate God, Jesus, who condescended so low for our sake that we may have a chance to reach Eternal Glory. How foolish we are when we put the lesser glories, fleeting glories first. How we continue to insult Jesus. Christians must turn back to Jesus, to adore, to love, to give thanks, to make reparation for so many insults. Like Veronica, we will express our love clearly and boldly.

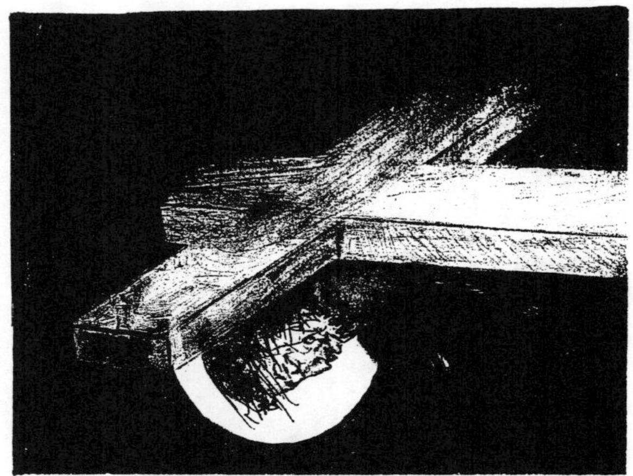

Seventh station. Jesus falls a second time.

He is showing us the magnitude of the punishment due to sin. Human frailty cannot bear it. Let us remember that there are too many sins and we should not add to them. Jesus, perfect God and perfect man could not carry that punishment with ease. Imagine if we had to do it all by ourselves! Why do we tend to remain distant from Him? What do we gain by being independent and for how long can we depend on ourselves when death is drawing nigh. God alone can give us true self-knowledge and the humility to abandon ourselves in his hands.

Eighth station. Jesus consoles the women of Jerusalem.

Wise women, simple women, with body and soul, recognized the reality before them, the pity of the ways of the common mankind, the ingratitude and insults toward God and they wept. Today, many people, modern people, are distracted and mystified by the enjoyment of technological and scientific advancement. Civilized people are ambitious for earthly glory to the extent of neglecting their own souls, and failing to perceive the truths of eternal life. Those truths are found along the way of the cross. There, Jesus speaks to us so intimately. May God make us quick to learn all that he teaches us.

Ninth station.   Jesus falls the third time.

Our sin is three times too heavy but God: the Father, Son and Holy Spirit has not wanted to hold it against us and has placed the weight on Jesus' shoulder. Jesus represents all men and women. He falls prostrate on our behalf. He suffers as a man, in place of the human sinner, but that suffering has infinite value because He is the same God. He satisfies the Father. He gains for mankind the Spirit. He is so identified with us that He is ready to do anything for us but we too often prefer to forget Him. We need to do all we can to be identified with him and to claim the redemption he won for us.

Tenth station.   Jesus is stripped of His garment.

How we continue to strip Jesus of what belongs to him and then we keep everything for ourselves. Our God is so patient, so merciful, and we are so foolish. No matter our gains in this world: honors, positions, fame, money, estates, children, friends - if we do not through all these seek the Glory of God, we are wasting our time. We are destined to suffer when all these are taken away from us at the moment of our death and if there is where we set our hearts, that suffering will never end for all eternity. Above all, we will suffer the loss of God our savior, having with our own doing stripped him of the claim to our soul. That claim is our share of His Glory predestined for us for He made us for Himself. It is never too late to restore our privileged destiny as long as we are alive.

Eleventh station.   Jesus is nailed to the cross.

Jesus, Eternal High Priest, mediator between God and people, offers Himself as a pleasing sacrifice – a holocaust wholly consumed for us all. The Lamb of God who takes away the sin of the world is still available for us today. We partake of that Holy Sacrifice each time we attend the Holy Mass "in remembrance of Him (Luke 22: 19)". There we receive His Body, given up for us, the Bread of Life so that we may live through Him, with Him, in Him, and the Holy Spirit giving all glory and honor to God our Almighty Father. How can we fail to participate in the Holy Mass as often as we can?

Twelfth station. Jesus dies on the cross.

Today, He lives. He has won the victory for us over sin, death and all the mysteries of life. It is left to each of us to claim that victory by uniting ourselves with him, in prayer, in Holy Communion and in other sacraments, in reading the Gospel and in imitating His life. We too will meet death along the way of the cross; death to man's sinful self and therefore life; the life of His victory in our soul. All Christians must learn to live in the reality of the victory of Christ, in the truth of the redemption.

Thirteenth station.   Jesus is laid in the arms of His Blessed Mother.

There is no human being that has ever loved Jesus like his mother did. She defied all dangers and stayed close to Him even beneath the cross at his crucifixion when his chosen apostles except John had all fled in fear. This woman can never be denied anything by Jesus her son. This is a grandeur of God's love: that a new Eve should gain the privileges the first Eve lost, and even more – the privilege of being the Daughter of God the Father, Mother of God the Son, Spouse of God the Holy Spirit; and all generations will call her blessed, and then tell her: "Mother, behold your children".

Fourteenth station.   Jesus is laid in the tomb.

We laid Him in a tomb, the best we could do after such a colossal betrayal. But He does not belong there. He rose again. He is the Resurrection and the Life. He wants us to join Him, not to remain where we do not belong. The redemption is ours.   Sin and ignorance should no longer separate us from God or from one another.   He is the Way, the Truth and the Life. He is the Good Shepherd, our Master, Healer and Teacher who has opened for us the path of salvation: the Way of the Cross, sanctified, glorified, made fruitful. Lord Jesus, thank you!

PRAYER TO LOVE THE HOLY CROSS

I adore you,
My Savior, Jesus.
I venerate your Holy Cross;
Not just wood
That raised you above,
But your very sacrifice of love.
Which I esteem
And thus implore:
Increase my share,
To love it more.
Though oft,
As in Gethsemane,
To drink that cup
Is hard for me;
Your very deed
Will spurn me on,
To VICTORY –
The one you won.
And, so identified
With Thee,
My joy will last
Eternally. Amen.

PRAYER FOR ACCEPTANCE OF SUFFERING

Lord, the cross is such a mystery,
But it is what you wish to bless me with.
My lot is like each person on earth's.
Sometimes, it seems to me the worst.
Toil, pain, loss, failure, adversities,
Want, loneliness, uncertainties;
These and all my incapacities,
Are mine - as your cross on Calvary.
Your will be done, your will be done;
But gentle Savior, in return,
Bless your servant with joy and holiness.
Make my heart to love and forgive.
May your lesson to me be timely learnt
That it may please you
To restore and increase
Those blessings which I do not deserve.
And if this cup will not pass me by;
Lord,
Store up my treasures up on high. Amen.

PRAYER IN TROUBLE

In all things, may the most holy,
The most just,
And the most loveable will of God
Be done, praised,
And exalted above all forever.
Your will be done, O Lord.
Your will be done.
The Lord has given,
The Lord has taken away;
Blessed be the name of the Lord. Amen.

PRAYER FOR DETACHMENT

Take from me Lord,
All that takes me from you.
Give me Lord,
All that leads to you.
Detach me Lord,
From myself
That I may give
My all to You. Amen.

PRAYER TO OUR LADY OF SORROWS
Holy Mother,
 Make me feel as you have felt.
 Make my soul to glow and melt
 With the love of Christ
 My Lord.
Holy Mother,
 Pierce me through
 In my heart,
 Each wound renew,
 Of my Savior crucified.
Let me share with you his pain,
 Who for all my sins was slain,
 Who for me, in torments died.
Let me mingle tears with you,
 Mourning him
 Who mourned for me
 All the days that I may live.
Let me to my latest breath,
 In my body bear the death
 Of that dying son of yours. Amen.

(Extracted from the *" Stabat Mater Dolorosa"*)

DEVOTION TO THE HOLY SPIRIT

It pays to meditate on these words of the Scriptures referring to the Holy Spirit - "Whom God has given to those that obey him" (Acts 5: 32).

1. "The Spirit of truth, Whom the world cannot accept" (John 14: 17).
2. "Those who are led by the Spirit of God: They are the children of God" (Romans 8: 14).
3. "Spirit of wisdom and understanding, right judgement and courage, knowledge and reverence, wonder and awe in the presence of God" (Isaiah 11: 2-3).
4. "He will teach you all things and remind you of all I said to you" (John 14: 26; 16: 12-14).
5. "He will dwell with you, and be in you" (John 14: 17).
6. "He will guide you to all truth" (John 16: 13)
7. "…the Spirit gives life" (2Cor. 3: 6).
8. "Where the Spirit of the Lord is, there is freedom" (2Cor. 3: 17).

9. "Whoever says anything against the Holy Spirit will not be forgiven" (Matt. 12: 32).

10. "The Spirit too helps us in our weakness, for we do not know how to pray as we ought" (Romans 8: 26).

11. He who searches hearts knows what the Spirit means, for the Spirit intercedes for the saints as God himself wills (Romans 8: 27).

12. The Spirit scrutinizes all matters, even the deep things of God (1Cor. 2: 10).

13. The Spirit we have received is not the world's spirit but God's Spirit, helping us to recognize the gifts he has given us (1Cor. 2: 12).

14. "Are you not aware that you are the temple of God, and that the Spirit of God dwells in you? If anyone destroys God's temple, God will destroy him. For the temple of God is holy and you are that temple" (1Cor. 3: 16-17).

VENI CREATOR
Come, Holy Spirit, Creator come,
  From thy bright heavenly throne!
  Come, take possession of our souls,
  And make them all thy own!
Thou who art called the Paraclete,
  Best gift of God above,
  The living spring, the living fire,
  Sweet unction and true love!
Thou who art sevenfold in thy grace,
  Finger of God's right hand.
  His promise, teaching little ones
  To speak and understand.
O guide our minds with thy blest light;
  With love our hearts inflame,
  And with thy strength which ne'er decays
  Confirm our mortal frame.
Far from us drive our hellish foe,
  True peace unto us bring,
  And through all perils guide us safe
  Beneath thy sacred wing.
Through thee may we the Father know,
  Through thee the Eternal Son,
  And thee the Spirit of them both;
  Thrice blessed three in one.
All glory to the Father be,

And to the risen Son;
The same to thee, O Paraclete,
While endless ages run. Amen.

A PRAYER TO THE HOLY SPIRIT
Breathe in me,
      O Holy Spirit,
That my thought may be holy.
Act in me,
      O Holy Spirit,
That my works may be holy.
Draw my heart,
      O Holy Spirit,
That I love only what is holy.
Strengthen me,
      O Holy Spirit,
To defend all that is holy.
Guard me,
      O Holy Spirit,
That I may always be holy. Amen.

SUBMISSION TO THE HOLY SPIRIT
Spirit of God, inform my actions;
Make me love like Christ my Lord.
Take control of all my passions;
Show me how to live your Word:

When to be still and when to stir,
When to be bold and when to defer,
When to be quiet and when to speak,
When to be strong and when to be weak,
When to sow and when to reap,
When to laugh and when to weep,
When to begin and when to end,
When to be friend and when to defend,
When to munch and when to fast,
When to be first and when to be last,
When to be far and when to be near,
When to dare and when to fear,
When to hasten and when to delay.
Take control by night and day.
As I journey to Heaven above,
Keep me on the Way the Cross.
Spirit of God, make me love;
Let your gifts be not a loss. Amen.

PRAYER TO KEEP FROM ERROR
Come O Holy Spirit;
Guide me in Your Truth.
Engrave Your Law in me:
The Law of Love,
The Law of the New Testament,
The Law of the Gospel,

The Faith of Christians,
The Way of Salvation,
The Fruit of Redemption.
Teach me Your Law:
The Law of Freedom,
The Law of Truth,
The Law of Grace,
The Beatitudes of Life,
The Wisdom of the Spirit,
The Way of the Cross.
Make it Lord always:
A light to my pathway,
A lamp to my feet.
Come O Holy Spirit;
Teach me Your Law! Amen.

LITANY TO THE HOLY SPIRIT

Lord, have mercy on us.
Christ, have mercy on us.
Lord, have mercy on us.

God the Father of	Have mercy
Heaven	On us
God the Son	"
God the Holy Spirit	"
Holy Trinity, one God	"
Divine Essence, one true	

God   "
Spirit of truth and
wisdom   "
Spirit of holiness and
justice   "
Spirit of understanding
and counsel   "
Spirit of love and joy   "
Spirit of peace and
patience   "
Spirit of longanimity and
meekness   "
Spirit of benignity and
goodness   "
Love substantial of the
Father and the Son   "
Love and life of saintly
souls   "
Fire ever burning   "
Living water to quench
the thirst of hearts   "
From all evil   Deliver us
                                       O Holy Spirit

From all impurity of soul
and body   "
From all gluttony and
sensuality   "
From all attachments to
things of the earth   "
From all hypocrisy and

pretence   "

From all imperfections
and deliberate faults   "

From self-love and self
judgement   "

From our own will   "

From slander   "

From deceiving our
neighbors   "

From our passions and
disorderly appetites   "

From our inattentiveness
to your holy inspirations   "

From despising little
things   "

From debauchery and
malice   "

From love of comfort
and luxury   "

From wishing to seek or
desire anything other
than you   "

From everything that
displeases you   "

Most loving Father,   Forgive us.
Divine Word,   Have pity on us.
Holy and Divine Spirit,   Leave us not until we are
                             in the presence of the
                             Divine Essence, Heaven
                             of heavens

Lamb of God, you take away
the sins of the world,   Send us the
                                Divine Consoler.
Lamb of God, you take away
the sins of the world,   Fill us with the
                                gifts of your Spirit.
Lamb of God, you take away
the sins of the world,   Make the fruits of the
                                Holy Spirit
                                Increase within us.
                        Amen.

Invocation:

        Come, O Holy Spirit, fill the hearts
of your faithful and enkindle in them the fire
of your love.
Send forth your Spirit and they will be
created
And you will renew the face of the earth.

Prayer:

  O God, who by the light of the Holy Spirit
did instruct the hearts of the faithful, grant
us in the same Spirit to be truly wise and
ever rejoice in his consolation.
Through Jesus Christ our Lord. Amen.

PENTECOST SEQUENCE

Come, Holy Spirit, come!
  From your celestial home;
  Shed a ray of light divine.
Come, Father of the poor!
  Come, source of all our store!
  Come, within our bosom shine!
You, of comforters the best;
  You, the soul's most welcome guest,
  Sweet refreshment here below;
In our labor, rest most sweet,
  Grateful coolness in the heat;
  Solace in the midst of woe.
O most blessed light divine,
  Shine within these hearts of yours,
  And our inmost being fill!
Where you are not, man has naught,
  Nothing good in deed or thought,
  Nothing free from taint of ill.
Heal our wounds, our strength renew;
  On our dryness pour your dew;
  Wash the stains of guilt away;
Bend the stubborn heart and will;
  Melt the frozen, warm the chill;
  Guide the steps that go astray.
On the faithful who adore,

And confess you, evermore,
  In your sevenfold gift descend;
Give them virtues sure reward;
  Give them your salvation, Lord;
  Give them joys that never end.
Amen.

 # THE VIRTUES 

The Christian life in us is matured through training in virtues by the help of grace and prayer. Every instance, every encounter, every situation of life calls for practice of virtue or demands an increase in virtue.

THEOLOGICAL VIRTUES
Faith Hope Charity *(1Cor. 13: 13)*

CARDINAL VIRTUES *(Wisdom 8: 7)*
Prudence Justice Fortitude Temperance

OTHER VIRTUES	CAPITAL SINS
Humility	Pride
Liberality	Covetousness
Chastity	Lust
Meekness	Anger
Temperance	Gluttony
Brotherly love	Envy
Diligence	Sloth

EVANGELICAL COUNSELS	*WORDLY ATTRACTIONS*
Poverty	Lure of the eyes
Chastity	Lure of the flesh
Obedience	Pride of life

SEVEN GIFTS OF THE HOLY SPIRIT
(Isaiah 11: 2,3)

"Since you have set your hearts on spiritual gifts, try to be rich in those that build up the Church" (1Cor. 14: 12).

Wisdom
Knowledge
Understanding
Piety
Counsel
The fear of the Lord
Fortitude

TWELVE FRUITS OF THE HOLY SPIRIT
(Gal. 5: 22)

Charity	Longanimity
Joy	Mildness
Peace	Faith
Patience	Modesty
Benignity	Continence
Goodness	Chastity

" ... The greatest of these is charity" (1Cor. 13: 13). "Over all these virtues put on love, which binds the rest together and makes them perfect" (Col. 3: 14). "Love covers all offences" (Proverbs 10: 12). "Charity covers a multitude of sins" (1Peter 4: 8; James 5: 20). "Love never fails" (1Cor. 13: 18). "Love... surpasses all knowledge" (Eph. 3: 19). "Love never wrongs the neighbour, hence love is the fulfilment of the law (Romans 13: 10; Gal. 5: 14). "Seek eagerly after Love" (1Cor. 14: 1).

CHARITY

Is patient
Is kind
Feels no envy
Is never perverse
   or proud
Never insolent
Does not claim its right
Cannot be provoked
Does not brood
   over an injury
Takes no pleasure
   in wrong doing
But rejoices at
   the victory of truth
Sustains, believes, hopes,
Endures to the last *(1Cor. 13: 4-7).*

CHARITY is the summit of all the virtues, the meeting point of all the virtues. All the virtues lead us to love. We need all the virtues in order to attain charity in a complete sense. For example, we need faith in order to find love worthwhile. We need prudence to judge the proper object of love, the end of love, the reason for love, the dictates of love, and the ways of love. We need justice to give all their due. We need fortitude to love those we find least attractive, incompatible, or those who we tend to envy or those who do not appreciate us. We need temperance to control our feelings, likes and dislikes and to be free to give our thoughts and attention to others, to share their joys and sorrows, to know and understand them and to be able to give of what we have to those who are in greater need. We need patience in order to overlook failings, to forgive, to endure and to suffer for the good of others. All the gifts and talents and virtues we have are worthwhile as far as they relate to CHARITY (1Cor. 13: 1-3). "Walk in Love" (Eph. 5: 2) and this makes us very like our Father God.

SIX SINS AGAINST THE HOLY SPIRIT
We should ask God frequently for the grace to avoid these sins always.

Presumption

Despair

Resisting known truth

Envy of another's spiritual good

Obstinacy in sin

Final impenitence

SINS CRYING TO HEAVEN FOR VENGEANCE
These sins spoil the beauty of human society and therefore we cannot be indifferent about them and should pray against them and do whatever we can to prevent them.

Willful murder (*Gen. 4)*

The sin of Sodom (Gen. 18)

Oppression of the poor (Exod. 2)

Defrauding laborers of wages (James 5).

WAYS OF SHARING GUILT OF SIN
We may be constantly at fault in these matters and unless we regularly examine ourselves on them, we would be blind to them. They are of special importance to anyone who has any measure of authority. It is not enough for each person to avoid committing sin. We have to make the path to sanctity easier for our neighbour.

Counsel
Praise/flattery
Command
Concealment
Consent
Partner in sin
Provocation
Silence
Defending the ill done

OBSTACLES TO SPIRITUAL LIFE	*REMEDIES*
Self love	Love of God
Lukewarmness	Prayer (Matt. 5: 48; 7: 7-11)
Worldly compensation	Detachment (Matt. 6: 19-21; 19: 23)
Routine and easy life	The cross and narrow way (Matt. 7: 13-14)

False prophets/ teachers	The Sacraments of the Catholic Church (Matt. 7: 15-20)
Insincerity	Examination of conscience (Matt. 7: 21-23)
Discouragement	Foundation on the Gospel (Matt. 7: 24-27)
Anxiety	Reliance on grace (Matt. 6: 31-34)

LOVE OF NEIGHBOUR

"Love thy neighbour as thyself" and you do well. According to St James, this is the royal law of the scriptures, the law of the Kingdom (James 2: 8). If we expect God's mercy, it is logical that we should not fail to show mercy to others. "It is mercy I want, not sacrifice" (Matt. 9: 13). "For judgement is without mercy to him who has not shown mercy; but mercy triumphs over judgement" (James 2: 13). God rewards kindness readily: "Then your light will break forth like the dawn, and your wound shall quickly be healed: Your vindication shall go before you, and the glory of the Lord shall be your guard. Then you shall call, and the Lord will answer, you shall cry for help, and he will say: Here I am"

(Isaiah 58: 8-9).   God wants us to CARE for our neighbour, to be our brother's keeper, which we can show in many practical details of:
> *Compassion*
> *Affection*
> *Respect*
> *Empathy*

as we practice the corporal and spiritual Works of Mercy.   "Happy is he who has regard for the lowly and the poor" (Psalm 41: 2).   "...as often as you did it for one of my least brothers, you did it for me" (Matt. 25: 40, 45; Mark 9: 41).   "He who loves his neighbour has fulfilled the law" (Romans 13: 8).   For this, we need a universal heart: "If you love those who love you, what merit is there in that?" (Matt. 5: 46).   Jesus, the Master, told us: "Therefore all that you wish men to do to you, even so do also to them; for this is the Law and the Prophets" (Matt. 7: 12). He explicitly left us that duty to love starting from the ones closest to us: "A new commandment I give to you, that you love one another: that as I have loved you, you also love one another.   By this will all men know that you are my disciples, if you have love for one another" (John 13: 34-35; 15: 12-17).   Love is therefore the hallmark and witness of Christianity. But: "Keep your deeds of mercy secret, and your father who sees in secret will repay you" (Matt. 6: 4). In this way Christians "store up heavenly treasure which neither moths nor rust corrode nor thieves break in and steal" (Matt. 6: 20).

SEVEN CORPORAL WORKS OF MERCY
Give food to the HUNGRY
Give drink to the THIRSTY
Clothe the NAKED
Harbor the HOMELESS
Visit the SICK
Visit the IMPRISONED
Bury the DEAD

SEVEN SPIRITUAL WORKS OF MERCY
CONVERT the sinner
INSTRUCT the ignorant
COUNSEL the doubtful
COMFORT the sorrowful
BEAR wrongs patiently
FORGIVE injuries
PRAY for the living and the dead

MORE VIRTUES

It is easy to practice virtues when they help us to achieve our own aims in life such as success in business, professional advancement, and various ambitions. However when they are imposed on us for the common good and for our own eternal good it is sometimes difficult to practice them. True virtue is characterised by:

> *who performs the act,*
> *why the act was performed;*
> *how the act was performed.*

Perfect virtue *is that performed by the one in communion with God, in order to please God and according to the laws of God. The saints have taught us that the foundation of all virtue is HUMILITY and the end of all virtue is CHARITY. Without these, our virtue is only fleeting, has no root, and its fruits cannot last. The following are virtues for every day life, which we should try to practice appropriately, and which we should be grateful for when we see them in other people.*

Patience	Constancy
Order	Transparency
Sincerity	Confidence
Goodwill	Perseverance
Tolerance	Responsibility
Magnanimity	Decency
Composure	Sociability
Industriousness	Flexibility

Truthfulness	Firmness
Naturalness	Optimism
Honor	Indefatigability
Nobility	Meekness
Loyalty	Fidelity
Decorum	Gratitude
Modesty	Youthfulness
Affability	Vigilance
Simplicity	Tenacity
Serenity	Tact
Magnificence	Steadfastness
Adaptability	Courage
Detachment	Mercy
Friendliness	Generosity
Determination	Patriotism
Courtesy	Solidarity
Benevolence	Versatility

SUMMARY OF CHRISTIAN DOCTRINE

SEVEN SACRAMENTS

BAPTISM	We become Christians (John 3: 5; Acts 19: 1-5)
CONFIRMATION	We receive the fullness of the Holy Spirit (Acts 1: 8, 2: 4, 8: 17, 19: 6)
HOLY EUCHARIST	We receive Jesus, the Bread of life (John 6: 49-59; Luke 22: 19-20)
PENANCE	We have our sins forgiven (John 20: 21-23)
ANOINTING OF THE SICK	We receive healing of soul and body (James 5: 14-15)
HOLY ORDER	We are given ministers to serve the Church (Luke 22: 19; Acts 6: 6; 1Tim. 4: 14; 2Tim. 1: 6)
MATRIMONY	A man and woman join together in Christian marriage (Matt. 19: 6)

TEN COMMANDMENTS OF GOD

It is important to meditate on these commandments frequently to see how we are keeping them because God said: "Here then, I have today set before you life and prosperity, death and doom. If you obey the commandments of the Lord, your God, which I enjoin on you today, loving him, and walking in his ways, and keeping his commandments, statutes and decrees, you will live and grow numerous, and the Lord, your God, will bless you ...I have set before you life and death, the blessing and the curse. Choose life then..." (Deut. 30: 15-16, 19). Jesus, Who came, not to abolish the Law and the prophets but to fulfil them assured us that they will never be obsolete: "until heaven and earth pass away, not the smallest letter of the Law...shall be done away with". (Matt. 5: 18). He summarised for us the whole Law: " 'You shall love the Lord your God, with your whole heart, with your whole soul, with all your mind and with all your strength'. This is the greatest and the first commandment. The second is like it: 'You shall love you neighbour as yourself'. On these two commandments the whole law is based" (Matt. 22: 35-40; Mark 12: 29-31). "This is worth more than any burnt offering or sacrifice" (Mark 12: 33). "...whoever breaks the least significant of these commandments and teaches others to do so shall be called least in the Kingdom of God. Whoever fulfils and teaches these commandments shall be great in the Kingdom of God" (Matt. 5: 19-20). The commandments are like the keys to the heart of God: "If you love me and obey the commands I give you, I will ask the Father and he will give you another Paraclete to be with you always" (John 15: 16), and to His Kingdom: "If you wish to enter life, keep the commandments" (Matt. 19: 17).   But we must remember what St. Paul calls it: "... a New Covenant, a covenant, not of a written law, but of spirit" (2Cor. 3: 6).

1. Thou shall not have strange gods before me. Thou shall not make to thyself any graven thing; nor the likeness of anything that is in heaven above, or in the earth beneath, nor of those things that are in the waters under the earth. Thou shalt not adore them nor serve them.
2. Thou shalt not take the name of the Lord thy God in vain.
3. Remember that thou keep holy the Sabbath day.
4. Honor thy father and thy mother.
5. Thou shalt not kill.
6. Thou shalt not commit adultery.
7. Thou shalt not steal.
8. Thou shalt not bear false witness against thy neighbour.

9. Thou shalt not covet thy neighbour's wife.

10. Thou shalt not covet thy neighbour's goods.

SIX CHIEF COMMANDMENTS OF THE CHURCH

1. To keep Sundays and holy days of obligation holy by hearing Mass and resting from servile work.
2. To keep the days of fasting and abstinence appointed by the Church.
3. To go to confession at least once a year.
4. To receive the Holy Eucharist at least once a year, at Easter or thereabouts.
5. To contribute to the support of the pastors.
6. Not to marry within certain degrees of kindred without dispensation.

INDULGENCES

Apart from eternal punishment, the justice and mercy of God also provide temporal (with a limit in time) punishment for sins. This punishment is what is 'lacking in the sufferings of Christ' (Col. 1: 24; 2Cor. 6: 10) - the contribution or co-operation of the guilty. We can only pay very little. Christ paid practically everything (2Cor. 5: 21; Col. 2: 13-15) and has made up for our inadequacy. But we must show our love for God and regret for all sin not just our own as far as we are adequate to do so (2Cor. 6: 4-10). Temporal punishment is therefore our lot as sinners.

The Church offers us indulgences i.e. removal of temporal punishment both here and in purgatory. Those on earth are however the only ones who can obtain indulgences for themselves and for the souls in purgatory.

A partial indulgence takes away part of the temporal punishment due to sin already forgiven. A plenary indulgence takes away all the punishment due to sins that have been forgiven.

A person who wants to receive an indulgence must be free from the guilt of mortal sin and must carry out the specified good works (usually to go to confession, receive Holy Communion and to pray for the Pope) or abstinence (e.g. from alcohol).

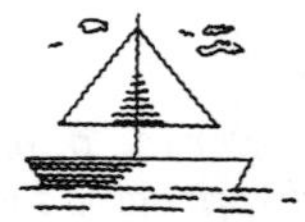

 # REMINDERS 

The interior life or supernatural life begins in baptism and is strengthened and matured by all the other sacraments, and by prayer, suffering and life experiences in the presence of God. Many things we know (or have) need to be renewed and increased in order for us to move closer to perfection. This is why for an ordinary maturing Christian, interior life is repeated beginnings: examination of conscience, discovery, resolution, struggle and conquest become - so to speak – the 'circadian rhythm'.

*Modern life however is so fast and so demanding on our psychic, energies and emotions that we are so restless. Many people cannot manage to be **ordinary people** plus **ordinary Christians.** Our brain, the hard drive that controls our activity as ordinary people is loaded and overloaded with all kinds of programs, files and folders of stuff to remember and things to do and often there isn't room any more for those things we need to remember to be ordinary Christians. This chapter is a floppy disc full of reminders. A peep inside and immediately you have some prayer bytes restored in the brain!*

Furthermore, these reminders may serve as:
-a useful guide for examination of conscience during a retreat
-to provide topics to spur us into conversation with God during our daily periods of prayer or meditation
-inspiration to struggle in particular aspects of life

-focus points to make resolutions regularly to keep our interior life active.

They are mainly from the wisdom of the scriptures, saints and also from great men and women of all ages.

Like St. Peter, "I intend to recall these things to you constantly, even though you already understand and are firmly rooted in the truth you possess" (2Peter 1: 12): may we prompt one another with useful reminders (2Peter 1: 13), so that goodness may abound: "A good man produces good from the store of goodness" (Matt. 12: 35).

SECTION I
ABOUT REALITY

1. A man reaps only what he sows (Gal. 6: 8).
2. A prayerful soul is a powerful person.
3. A soul of prayer need not be concerned about the devil.
4. Action speaks louder than words.
5. All problems are artificial.
6. An evil and unfaithful age is eager for a sign (Matt. 16: 4, 12: 39).
7. Anyone who is not against us is with us (Mark 9: 40; Luke 9: 50).
8. As the family goes, so goes the nation (John Paul II).
9. Bad company corrupts good morals (1Cor. 15: 33).
10. Basic requirement: faith in Jesus Christ (Gal. 3: 26).
11. Because of the increase of evil, the love of most will grow cold (Matt. 24: 12).

12.   Beware of Satan who cannot do good and would try to undo anything good.
13.   Blest are they who have not seen and have believed (John 20: 29).
14.   Both in life and in death we are the Lord's (Romans 14: 8).
15.   Charity is the mother of all virtues.
16.   Christ has won the victory.
17.   Christ left a hierarchy for His Church not to be anarchy (cf. Matt. 16: 18-19; 28: 18-20; Luke 10: 16; John 21: 15-17).
18.   Conscience: continuous.
19.   Constant presence of God.
20.   Dangers: sin, error, ignorance.
21.   Devil's delight: virtuous atheists and sinful Christians.
22.   Do good to all men (Gal. 6: 10).
23.   Do not condemn and you will not be condemned (Luke 6: 37).
24.   Do not hide moral truths spread them!
25.   Do not judge and you will not be judged (Luke 6: 37; Romans 14: 10, 13).

26. Do to others what you will have them do to you (Luke 6: 13).
27. Don't be afraid of those who kill the body and can do no more (Luke 12: 4).
28. Don't judge by appearances (John 7: 24).
29. Eternity is reality.
30. Even legitimate demands of the flesh can be given up (1Cor. 15: 36).
31. Even the devil knows the scriptures (Matt. 4: 3-11).
32. Ever effective chastisement: Love.
33. Every one who lives in sin is the slave of sin (John 8: 34).
34. Every sin, not only terrible sin, offends God.
35. Every soul needs an outlet.
36. Everyone of us will have to give an account of himself before God (Romans 14: 12).
37. Faith is above reason.
38. Faith is the substance of things to be hoped for, the evidence of things that are not seen (Hebrews 11:1).

39. False churches, false philosophies, false advisers - add to our miseries.
40. False prophets will appear performing signs and wonders (Matt. 24: 24).
41. False prophets will rise in great numbers to mislead many (Matt. 24: 11).
42. Give men freedom and the thinker will think best, the writer write best, the saint will pray best and the sinner will sin best.
43. Go for spiritual direction frequently.
44. God can raise children from stones and money from nowhere.
45. God arranges things.   Let the will of God be.
46. God does not contradict Himself.
47. God exists (Ex. 3: 14).
48. God is a God, not of confusion, but of peace.
49. God is a father with a "left hand" and a "right hand" to punish and to bless.
50. God is always looking after us.
51. God is clear (cf. Romans 1: 19; 1Cor. 14: 33).

52.   God is great.
53.   God is light (1John 1: 5).
54.   God is love (John 4: 8, 16).
55.   God is Lord of Cosmos.
56.   God is more generous than we are.
57.   God is my friend.
58.   God is our Father (cf. Matt. 23: 9;
       Luke 12: 30).
59.   God is rich in mercy (Eph.2: 4).
60.   God is spirit and those who worship
       him must worship in spirit and in
       truth (John 4: 23-24).
61.   God is trustworthy (1Cor. 1: 9).
62.   God knows best.
63.   God's 'foolishness' is wiser than
       human wisdom (1Cor. 1: 22).
64.   God looks at the heart (1Sam. 16: 7).
65.   God tests us to make us strong; the
       devil and his agents tempt us to
       make us weak.
66.   God wants all men to be saved and to
       come to know the truth (1Tim. 2: 3-
       4).
67.   Grace does not destroy nature (Frank
       Sheed).
68.   Greatest feat: overcoming sin.

69.   Great sinners can make great saints
        (cf. Luke 7: 47).
70.   Great things are made up of little
        things.
71.   He has made you little less than a
        god (Psalm 8: 6) but don't be a god.
72.   He who loses his life…will find it
        (cf. Matt. 10: 39).
73.   His delight is to be with the children
        of men (cf. Proverbs 8: 31).
74.   His goodness is so good, we must be
        grateful.
75.   His sun rises on the bad and the
        good, he rains on the just and the
        unjust (Matt. 5: 45).
76.   How hard it will be for the rich to go
        into the Kingdom of God! (Luke 18:
        24; Mark 10: 23).
77.   Human intellect is grand and limited.
78.   Idolatry is not to accept God for
        what He is and does.
79.   Idolatry is to replace God with
        something else.
80.   Idolatry still abounds!
81.   If we are too busy doing good, we
        cannot do evil.

82. In Christ there is every ideal.
83. In the Lord's eyes, one day is as a thousand years (2Pet. 3: 8).
84. It is a wicked generation that asks for a sign (Matt. 12: 39, 16: 4).
85. It is proper of the wise to govern and judge.
86. It is safer to stand by the truth than to stand by men.
87. It is worthwhile to be faithful to God.
88. Jesus is Master of masters.
89. Jesus is the Way (John 14:6).
90. Let no one mislead you (Matt. 24: 4).
91. Like it or not: "Every knee shall bend… every tongue shall give praise to God" (Isaiah 45: 23-24; Phil. 2: 10-11; Romans 14: 11).
92. Limited vision: earthly comfort and progress.
93. Little is forgiven one whose love is small (Luke 7: 47).
94. Love Our Lady like the saints did.
95. Malice is dangerous; frustrated malice is deadly.
96. Malice is never superficial.
97. Man has no distance from the cross.

98. Man solves the problems God permits Him to solve.
99. Many do not know the depths of Satan (Rev. 2: 24).
100. Mary is the shortcut to Jesus (John 2: 1-11).
101. Maturity is the full development of all virtues.
102. Maturity is to give glory to God in all things.
103. Maturity is to live in reality.
104. Miracles, signs: only for supernatural reasons (Mark 16: 20).
105. Money, sex and power give pleasures too small and fleeting for a saint.
106. Mortification is all round: mind, heart, will and flesh.
107. Naked I came (Job 1: 21).
108. No freedom, no merit.
109. No prophet is without honor except in his own house (Matt 13: 57).
110. No sin is worthwhile.
111. Nobody plans to fail but many fail to plan (popular literature).

112. Not on bread alone does man live but on every utterance that comes from the mouth of God (Matt. 4: 4; Luke 4: 4).
113. Not to love God is a curse (1Cor. 16: 22).
114. Obedience to the hierarchy left by Jesus is obedience to Jesus (Luke 10: 16; John 21: 15-17).
115. Old age is not the only time for God.
116. One who is earthly speaks on an earthly plane (John 3: 31).
117. Only with difficulty will a rich man enter the Kingdom of God (Matt. 19: 23; Mark 10: 23; Luke 12: 15)
118. Our God forgives and gives.
119. Our parents, in spite of everything, are our parents (Luke 2: 51).
120. Our deeds are clearer than words.
121. Our widow's mite is our everything (Luke 21: 1-4).
122. Please God rather than men (1Thess. 2: 4).
123. Pray with the Gospel.
124. Prayerless life is wasteful life.

125.   Pretty ladies, good ladies are often prey of evil men.

126.   Read the Bible with love and respect.

127.   Remember the splendor of truth.

128.   Reparation means first to avoid sin.

129.   Rich men, powerful men are often prey of evil women.

130.   Satan took possession of Judas…a member of the twelve (Luke 22: 3).

131.   Saying part of the truth can be the greatest lie.

132.   Science and technology cannot replace God.

133.   Science is natural knowledge, faith is supernatural knowledge. Small fools reject science. Great fools reject faith.

134.   Simplicity is the salt of perfection (Blessed Josemaria).

135.   Sin always complicates our lives.

136.   Some sinners may die as saints and some saints may die as sinners.

137.   Sources of failure: error, ignorance, and confusion.

138.   Sundays are for pious rest not idleness.

139.   Tax collectors and prostitutes are entering the Kingdom of God before some dedicated people (cf. Matt. 21: 31).
140.   *Tempus breve est.* Time is short.
141.   The best we wait for may be the enemy of the good we have.
142.   The best time never comes.
143.   The best worship to God is the Holy Mass.
144.   The Church (One, Holy, Catholic, and Apostolic) is the pillar and bulwark of truth.   (cf. 1 Tim 3: 15).
145.   The cross dwells more in people than in the relic, we must venerate it with our lives.
146.   The daily miracles are all God's doings: the spectacular miracles may be God's; may be Satan's.
147.   The devil does not mind you keeping the nine if you would only break the first commandment.
148.   The devil does nothing for nothing.
149.   The devil is a liar and the father of lies (John 8: 44).

150.   The devil is envious of each man on earth because we still have a chance.

151.   The devil is real, but really less than nothing.

152.   The devil is so unbelievable!

153.   The devil prowls around like a roaring lion looking for someone to devour (1Pet. 5: 8).

154.   The devil's agents can quote the gospels as well as saints.

155.   The devil's consolations are smug agnostics, bold atheists and lukewarm Christians.

156.   The earth is the Lord's and its fullness thereof (1Cor. 10: 26).

157.   The flesh lusts against the spirit and the spirit against the flesh (Gal. 5: 17).

158.   The fool says in his heart, "there is no God" (Psalm 14: 1).

159.   The good leader respects freedom, conscience and grace.

160.   The gospel is superior to any other book.

161.   The greatest sin – idolatry:
       egocentric, humanistic, materialistic
       idolatry.
162.   The Holy Eucharist is a memorial, a
       real memorial, a reality.
163.   The Holy Mass – a miracle at hand
       for all each day.
164.   The human intellect can achieve
       greatness and with grace can achieve
       much more.
165.   The invited are many, the elect are
       few (Matt. 22: 14).
166.   The Kingdom of God is extended to
       all men (Acts 2: 21; 2Peter 3: 9;
       Titus 2: 11).
167.   The Kingdom of God is within you
       (Luke 17: 21).
168.   The less we pray, the more we need
       our pride and pleasures.
169.   The life of man upon earth is
       warfare. (Job 7: 1).
170.   The love of God consists in this: that
       we keep His commandments…which
       are not burdensome (1John 5: 3).
171.   The marriage bed is an altar and not
       a gutter (Blessed Josemaria).

172. The Mass is the center and root of our interior life (Blessed Josemaria).

173. The more perfect we strive to be the more grace can dwell in us.

174. The new law is a law of love, of grace and of freedom.

175. The one who lacks love lacks authority.

176. The peaceful pain, the purifying pain, the best pain, the sanctifying pain; the pain that matters, glorifying pain is the pain of restraining oneself from sin.

177. The planner makes use of order, the opportunist makes use of disorder.

178. The Pope succeeds St. Peter as the Head of the Church (cf. Matt. 16: 17–19).

179. The prince of this world is already condemned (John 16: 11).

180. The reality of life is there is only one law – love (cf. Galatians 5: 14).

181. The ruler is God's servant to work for your good (Romans 13: 4).

182. The saints will shine like the sun in their Father's Kingdom (Matt. 13: 43).
183. The sinless should cast the first stone (John 8: 7).
184. The source of our joy is our guarantee of Heaven (Luke 10: 20).
185. The spirit is willing but nature is weak (Matt. 26: 21).
186. The truth shines.
187. The truth will set you free (John 8: 32).
188. The whole creation is affected by sin (cf. Romans 8: 20-22).
189. The whole man, renewed man is achieved by the grace of God who made man.
190. The Word of God is living and active (Heb. 4: 12).
191. The Word of God will never be obsolete (Luke 21: 33).
192. The world is too short of charity.
193. There are few who pray and they pray little.
194. There is a reason for everything.

195.   There is no greater love than this: to lay down one's life for one's friends (John 15: 13).

196.   There is no pleasure without sufferings.

197.   There is one mediator between God and men, himself man, Christ Jesus (1Tim.2: 5).

198.   There is only one peace: the peace of the Reign of God.

199.   There is only one true Church – the catholic – with its hierarchy established by Christ (cf. Matt. 16: 18-19, 28: 18-20).

200.   There is only one unity, the unity of the Reign of God.

201.   There will be only one flock (cf. John 17: 11, 21, 23).

202.   Those who are in union with Christ are in union with Mary, the Angels and Saints, the Pope and priests and entire church.

203.   Those who are truthful are quick and sure paths to progress.

204. Those who like to share your joys
      can be trusted to truly share your
      sorrows (cf. Romans 12: 15).
205. Those who love Christ also love
      Mary, the Saints, the Pope, the
      priests and His whole Mystical
      Body.
206. Those who reached perfection gave
      everything to God (cf. Matt. 19: 21;
      Luke 12: 33).
207. Those who use the sword are sooner
      or later destroyed by it (Matt. 26:
      52).
208. Time is glory (Blessed Josemaria).
209. To be holy, be *essentially Christian.*
210. To gain everything, gain charity.
211. To know how to live, we must know
      how to love.
212. Tradition must not go against God
      (cf. Matt. 15: 3; Mark 7: 8).
213. True love: universal heart.
214. Unless the grain of wheat falls to the
      earth and dies, it remains just a grain
      of wheat (John 12: 24).
215. Unless the Lord builds, in vain do we
      build (Matt. 15: 13).

216. Vanities of vanities, all is vanity (cf. Eccles. 1: 2).
217. Vices clump together, so do virtues.
218. We are all called to holiness (Ephesians 1: 4).
219. We are made by God's power and to His glory.
220. We are more than conquerors (Romans 8: 37).
221. We are often compelled to choose flesh or spirit (Romans 8: 5, 13).
222. We have limitations but grace does not.
223. We must acknowledge God.
224. We must encourage worship - with rigid ritual or spontaneous spirit - we must encourage worship.
225. We must have faith in all those who can show us the truth (Mark 16: 14).
226. We must suffer with Christ (Romans 8: 17).
227. We need family, of the blood, of the spirit (Luke 2: 16; Romans 1: 9-13).
228. What can a man offer in exchange of himself? (Matt. 16: 26; Mark 8: 37).

229.   What have you that you have not
        received? (1Cor. 4: 7).
230.   What terrible things will come on the
        world through scandal (Matt 18: 7;
        Romans 1: 31).
231.   Whoever are led by the Spirit of
        God, they are the sons of God
        (Romans 8: 14).
232.   Whoever is of God hears every word
        God speaks (John 8: 47).
233.   Without courage, there is no
        overcoming sin.
234.   Work is the hinge of our sanctity
        (Blessed Josemaria).
235.   Worship is the only true gift of man
        to God.
236.   You always have sins - go to
        confession frequently.
237.   You are important and necessary.
238.   You are the temple of God (1Cor. 3:
        16; 2Cor. 6: 16).
239.   You can tell a tree by its fruits (Matt.
        7: 20).
240.   You can't be too modern to be
        Christian.

241.	You cannot tell by careful watching when the reign of God will come (Luke 17: 20).

242.	You err because you do not know the scriptures nor the power of God. (Matt. 22: 29).

243.	You have been ransomed at a great price (1Cor. 6: 20, 7: 23).

244.	You have to live as Christ taught us to live.

245.	You have to know what love is for you to know what it isn't.

246.	You may get full measure, pressed down and flowing over (Luke 6: 38).

247.	Your body is not yours (Romans 12: 1-2; 1Cor. 6: 19).

248.	Your failure in one thing is your success in another.

249.	Your sins are already enough (cf. 1Pet. 4: 3).

250.	You shall not put the Lord your God to the test (Matt. 4: 7; Luke 4: 12).

 ## SECTION II
FOR SUPPORT

1.   About failing - be truly and immediately sincere.
2.   All will soon be over.
3.   Always on the narrow road.
4.   Anchor yourself in Christ (cf. Colossians 2: 7).
5.   Ask and you will receive. Seek and you will find. Knock and it will be opened to you (Matthew 7: 7; Luke 11: 9).
6.   Ask God (John 6: 45).
7.   Be a permanent learner.
8.   Be assiduous in prayer (Col. 4: 2).
9.   Be careful to do what is right (Titus 3: 8).
10. Be conditioned only by the love and freedom of the children of God.
11. Be faithful unto death (Rev. 2: 10).
12. Be madly in love with Jesus Christ.
13. Be still and know that I am God.
14. Be subject to authority (Titus 3: 1).
15. Be unshakeable in all that is good.

16.   Be wise as serpents and simple as doves (cf. Matt. 10: 16).
17.   Bear in mind, the image of Christ.
18.   Bear the sins of others as Christ did. (cf. Hebrews 9: 28).
19.   Bear yourself blameless in His presence.
20.   Before God, listening abandonment.
21.   Before God, men should nod their heads and bow.
22.   Begin and begin again (Blessed Josemaria).
23.   Bless those who curse you and pray for those who maltreat you (Luke 6: 28; Romans 12: 14).
24.   Blest are those who hear the word of God and keep it (Luke 11: 28).
25.   Call the name of Jesus (cf. Acts 2: 21, 3: 6, 16, 4: 10-12; Romans 10: 13).
26.   Carry the good spirit of Christ (cf. 2Cor. 2: 15)
27.   Cast all your cares upon him (1Peter 5: 7).
28.   Challenges make us strong, better and more matured.

29.   Charity unites.
30.   Children of God! That is what we
       are! (1John 3: 1).
31.   Constantly rely on grace.
32.   Correct your brother charitably
       (Matt. 18: 15-17; Luke 17: 9).
33.   Create a virtuous circle.
34.   Creatures cannot mortify us.
35.   Demands of the flesh – pure or
       impure – can be controlled.
36.   Do everything with love (1Cor. 16:
       14).
37.   Do good to those who hate you
       (Luke 6: 27).
38.   Do not be afraid! (Matt. 14: 27, 28:
       10; Mark 5: 36; Luke 12: 4, 12, 32;
       John 6: 20).
39.   Do not be anxious about your life
       (Luke 12: 22-31).
40.   Do not be ashamed of Christ and His
       Gospel (Mark 8: 38; Luke 12: 9;
       Romans 1: 16).
41.   Do not be conquered by evil but
       conquer evil with good (Romans 12:
       21).
42.   Do not create needs.

43.   Do not resist the evildoer (cf. Luke 27: 30).
44.   Do not try to save your life (John 12: 25; Matt. 16: 25; Mark 8: 35; Luke 9: 24).
45.   Do whatever he tells you (John 2: 5).
46.   Don't be a gorilla - smile.
47.   Don't be afraid of the devil or his agents.
48.   Don't be afraid of the truth.
49.   Don't be ashamed to be miserable - offer all to God sincerely.
50.   Don't be offended. God is the one offended.
51.   Don't forget His benefits.
52.   Don't get overwhelmed (cf. 2Cor. 12: 10).
53.   Don't neglect His grace.
54.   Drown evil in abundance of good (Blessed Josemaria).
55.   Each should be certain of his own conscience (Romans 14: 5).
56.   Each suffering is a participation in the mystery of the redemption.
57.   *Ecce homo!* Behold the man! Look at Jesus! (cf. John 19: 5).

58.   Enter through the narrow gate (Matt. 7: 13).

59.   Esteem: the will of God and the way of the cross.

60.   Eucharistic soul: through Him, with Him, in Him (cf. Phil. 1: 6).

61.   Even if last in everything: be first in love.

62.   Even sinners love those who love them (Luke 6: 32).

63.   Every hair on your head has been counted (Matt. 10: 30; Luke 12: 22).

64.   Faith is effective today, now, no other time.

65.   Faith is needed where reason cannot cope.

66.   Faith is what counts (Gal. 5: 6; Eph. 6: 16).

67.   Faith moves mountains (cf. Mark 11: 23-24).

68.   Fear is useless, what is needed is trust (Mark 5: 36).

69.   For those who believe, all things are possible (cf. Mark 10: 27, 11: 24).

70.   For those who do not pray – the devil is a winner.

71. Forgive - not seven times but seventy times seven times (Matt. 18: 22, 35; Luke 17: 4).

72. Frequent retreat is necessary (Mark. 6: 32, 46; Luke 5: 16, 6: 12).

73. From Him, through Him, for him (Romans 11: 36).

74. Godly life? Expect persecution (2Tim. 3: 12).

75. Good is always stronger than evil.

76. Have salt in yourself and be at peace with one another. (Mark 9: 49)

77. He does not treat us according to our sins (cf. Ezk. 33: 11).

78. He is powerful and more than powerful enough.

79. He who abides in love abides in God (John 4: 16).

80. Heaven is watching you.

81. Holiness cannot be blocked by obstacles. Obstacles - jump over, go round, dig under, hack it down - be a go-getter.

82. Hope for the best, expect the worst.

83. I am a member of the body of Christ (1Cor. 12: 27).

84.   I laugh at my weakness.
85.   If God is for us who can be against us? (Romans 8: 31).
86.   If we want more grace, we must have more purification.
87.   If you are not praying all the time, you are losing all the time.
88.   If you wish to enter life, keep the commandments (Matt. 19: 17).
89.   Imagine the Cross.
90.   In all you do remember the end of your life (Sirach 7: 36; cf. Matt. 15: 13; Luke 12: 19-20).
91.   In each situation ask: what did Christ do while on earth, what should a saint do in this case?
92.   In Him we live and move and have our being (Acts 17: 28).
93.   In the Name of Jesus (John 14: 14).
94.   In want or abundance, we are equally happy (Phil. 4: 11-12).
95.   Insist on doing good.
96.   Insults? Jesus has more.
97.   It is better to give than to receive (Acts 20: 35).
98.   It is God who rules the world.

99. It is when we go lowest that God takes us highest.

100. Joy always.

101. Joy has its roots in the shape of a cross (Blessed Josemaria).

102. Keep his commandments (1John 2: 3).

103. Keeping his commandments is perfect love (cf. 1John 2: 5).

104. Laugh at everything.

105. Learn to wait for God.

106. Life is a new song each day.

107. Live the Communion of Saints.

108. Living virtues, growing virtues.

109. Livingstone, edifice of spirit (cf. 1Peter 2: 5).

110. Look and learn.

111. Love and do what you will (St. Augustine of Hippo).

112. Love and knowledge of God: these suffice (Hosea 6: 1-6).

113. Love covers a multitude of sins (1Peter 4: 8).

114. Love has no room for fear (1John 4: 18).

115. Love knows wisdom.

116. Love one another (John 13: 34).
117. Love your enemies (Luke 6: 27).
118. Make every effort to be found without stain or defilement and at peace in his sight (2Peter 3: 14).
119. Make love your reference.
120. Make up for defects of other people.
121. Many who are first shall come last, and the last shall come first (Matt. 19: 30).
122. Meditate on the Gospel.
123. Mention the little things in spiritual direction.
124. Mortification prevents penance.
125. Never be scandalized.
126. Never compare.
127. Never repay injury with injury (Romans 12: 17).
128. No cross, no crown.
129. No one who believes in him will be put to shame (Romans 10: 11; cf. Sirach 2: 11).
130. No servant is greater than the Master. (Matt. 10: 24; John 13: 16; 15: 20).

131. Not by fire, not by sword - by the spirit of the Lord.
132. Nothing is concealed that will not be revealed (Matt. 10: 26).
133. Nothing is impossible with God (Luke 1: 37).
134. Obey your leaders and submit to them (Heb. 13: 17; 1Peter 2: 13).
135. Obstacles will only make us stronger (Blessed Josemaria).
136. Offer no resistance to God.
137. *Omnia in bonum*. All things work together for good (Romans 8: 28).
138. One track mind - child of God.
139. Our sufferings purify us for Heaven.
140. Pain? As on Calvary!
141. Pardon and you shall be pardoned (Luke 6: 37).
142. Pass through the agony of struggling against sin.
143. Patience pays (Yoruba proverb).
144. Peace is the tranquillity that results from order (St. Augustine).
145. Peace is work of justice and effect of charity.

146.   Peace, God's peace is beyond all
        understanding (Phil. 4: 7).
147.   Play the role of a saint.
148.   Poverty does more good than harm.
149.   Poverty? As in Bethlehem!
150.   Poverty? With order, with clean-
        liness.
151.   Pray about everything (cf. Luke 2:
        19; Luke 11: 9; Col. 4: 2-4).
152.   Pray through temptations.
153.   Pray with attention and intentions.
154.   Prayer simplifies things.
155.   Prayer, interior sensitivity, spiritual
        finesse.
156.   Prayer: as in the wilderness, as on
        the mountain, as on Mount Thabor,
        as in Gethsemani, as on Calvary (cf.
        Mark 1: 35, 6: 46; Luke 5: 16, 6: 12;
        Matt. 26: 39, 27: 46).
157.   Put on the Lord Jesus Christ
        (Romans 13: 14).
158.   Put your trust in God (cf. Mark 11:
        22; Luke 12: 4).
159.   Read the Bible (cf. Acts 17: 11).
160.   Real virtue shines through.

161.   Rejoice - the Lord is at hand
        (Philippians 4: 5).
162.   Rejoice in the Lord always
        (Philippians 4: 4).
163.   Rejoice to suffer (1Peter 4: 13; cf.
        Romans 8: 17).
164.   Relax - don't be a teddy bear.
165.   Rely on grace (cf. 2 Cor. 12: 9).
166.   Restraining oneself from sin is more
        worthwhile than the costliest act of
        reparation and penance.
167.   See that your conduct is honorable in
        the eyes of all (Romans 12: 17).
168.   Self-abandonment.
169.   Shame: only to sin again.
170.   Sift everything in prayer.
171.   Sincerely prefer good to evil
        (Romans 12: 6).
172.   Sincerely prefer truth to falsehood
        (cf. 2Thess. 2: 10-12).
173.   Slowly but surely (Irish proverb).
174.   Stay awake and sober (1Thess. 5: 6).
175.   Stay close to your guardian angel.
176.   Stress? Fears? God supports (cf.
        2Cor. 7: 5-6)
177.   Strive for all the virtues.

178.   Take care to grow in charity (cf.
        1Cor. 13: 1-7).
179.   Take care you do not forget the Lord.
        (Deut. 6: 4-13).
180.   Test everything: retain what is good.
181.   Thank God (Eph. 5: 20).
182.   The busier you are the more you
        need interior life.
183.   The cross will pain till you carry it.
184.   The devil keeps putting obstacles,
        which God allows to train us in
        virtues.
185.   The holocaust.
186.   The Holy Spirit will inspire us when
        we need it (Mark 13: 11; Luke 12:
        12).
187.   The holocaust.
188.   The Holy Spirit will inspire us when
        we need it (Mark 13: 11; Luke 12:
        12).
189.   The joy of the Lord is my strength.
190.   The just are the free.
191.   The just man lives by faith (Hebrews
        10:38; Gal. 3: 11; Romans 9: 32).
192.   The justice of God is my bliss.
193.   The liar too uses the truth.

194.   The Lord is my Shepherd (Psalm 23:
        1).
195.   The Lord's Will be done (Acts 21:
        14).
196.   The man who hates his brother is in
        darkness (1John 2: 11).
197.   The most cherished ambition -
        sanctity.
198.   The only thing I can boast about is
        the cross of Our Lord Jesus Christ
        (cf. Gal. 6: 14).
199.   The path of virtue is difficult to
        nature, easy to grace (Venerable
        Louis of Granada).
200.   The prince of this world has been
        condemned (John 16: 11).
201.   The sufferings of the good man are
        rewarding (1Peter 4: 13-16).
202.   The truth shall set you free (John 8:
        32).
203.   The truth will out (cf. Mark 4: 22).
204.   The way of the cross is far easier
        than what men suffer living in sin.
205.   There is nothing concealed that will
        not be revealed (Matt. 10: 26; Mark
        4: 22; Luke 12: 3).

206. There is nothing I shall want (Psalm 23: 1).

207. Things are hidden only to be revealed at a later time (Mark 4: 22; Luke 8: 17).

208. Things are means - not more.

209. Things go better with prayer (Mark 9: 29).

210. Think - how would Jesus have done it?

211. Those who have will get more… those who have not will lose even the little they have (Matt. 25: 29).

212. Those who know the cross are never seen suffering.

213. Through Jesus Christ (Luke 10: 22).

214. Through mortification we will have fewer sins to do penance for.

215. Time will prove where wisdom lies (Matt. 11: 19).

216. To live one must die (John 12: 24).

217. Truly fear God.

218. Truth is the quick and sure path to progress.

219. Try to judge by God's standards not by man's (Matt. 16: 23; Romans 2: 3-4).
220. Turn the other cheek (Luke 6: 29).
221. Unless a grain of wheat falls...and dies, it remains just a grain of wheat (John 12: 24).
222. Vengeance belongs to God (Rom. 12: 19).
223. We all have weak points.
224. We are all learners. God is our Teacher (Matt. 23: 8).
225. We cannot be envious because God is generous to others (Matt 20: 15).
226. We live as we pray.
227. We would often resort to prayer (Mark 9: 29).
228. What charity dictates is more important than what human laws permit.
229. Whatever you do, do for the glory of God (cf. 1Cor. 10: 31).
230. When I am powerless, it is then that I am strong (2Cor. 12: 10).
231. When we begin to forgive, we begin to be rich (Mark 11: 24-25).

232. Where there is a will there is a way
      (popular literature).
233. Who are you to answer God back?
      (Romans 9: 20).
234. Whoever humbles himself shall be
      exalted (Matt. 23: 12).
235. Whoever makes himself like a child,
      is great in the Kingdom of Heaven
      (cf. Matt. 18: 4; Mark 10: 15).
236. Whoever would save his life would
      lose it (Matt16: 25).
237. Whom the Lord loves, he disciplines
      (Heb. 12: 6; cf. Rev. 3:19).
238. With joy no day without the cross.
      (Blessed Josemaria).
239. With God, a thousand years are like
      one day (2Peter 3:8).
240. Words of wisdom - let it be (Luke 1:
      38).
241. You are important and necessary in
      the human family.
242. You are more than a conqueror
      (Romans 8: 37).
243. You have to live as Christ taught us
      to live.

244.   You have to sacrifice the fallen
        nature to enjoy the new life of glory.
245.   You must wash each other's feet
        (John 13: 14).
246.   You will receive all that you pray for
        provided you have faith (Matt. 21:
        22).
247.   Your joy, no one shall take from you
        (John 16: 27).
248.   Your persecutors: bless and do not
        curse them (cf. Romans 12: 14).

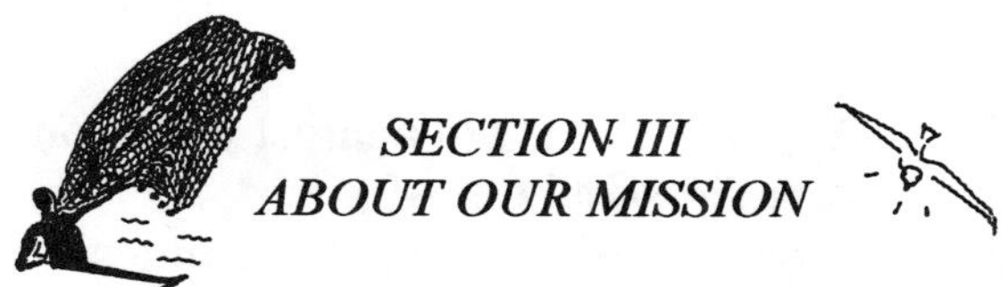

SECTION III
ABOUT OUR MISSION

1. A eunuch for the Kingdom (Matt. 19: 12).
2. A friend indeed.
3. Accursed be that man by whom the Son of Man is betrayed (Mark 14: 21).
4. Administrator, be trustworthy (1Cor. 4: 2).
5. Admonish sinners (Luke 17: 3).
6. All for the glory of God (1Cor. 10: 31).
7. All men have sinned and are deprived of the glory of God (Romans 3: 10, 3: 23).
8. All things to all men in order to save (1Cor. 9: 22).
9. Always dialogue never monologue with God or fellow men.
10. Among you…… there will be false teachers (2Peter 2: 1).
11. Anticipate your neighbours' needs.

12. Anyone who is not against you is on your side (Luke 9: 49).

13. Anyone…who aspires to greatness must serve the rest (Matt. 20: 26).

14. Apostolate – bearing witness, must be both personal and collective; private and public (cf. Acts 20: 20; Macc. 6:18-31).

15. As for me and my house, we will serve the Lord. (Josh. 24: 1-5, 15-18)

16. Ask for the Holy Spirit (cf. Luke 11: 13; John 4: 5-42).

17. A sure means for directing souls is personal sanctity.

18. At all times – vigilance (Acts 20: 30).

19. Avoid any semblance of evil (2Thess. 3: 6, 5: 22; 1Peter 2: 1).

20. Avoid scandal (Romans 14: 21, 16: 17; 2Cor. 6: 3).

21. Be as free as truth is truth.

22. Be correct in your judgement of what pleases the Lord (Eph. 5: 10).

23. Be ready for every grace, every inspiration, every conversion, the Second Coming of Christ, death.
24. Be steady and self-possessed (2Tim. 4: 5).
25. Better obey God than men (Acts 5: 29).
26. Care for the truth.
27. Carry the cross with the dignity of love.
28. Carry the sweet odor of Christ (cf. 2Cor. 2: 15).
29. Celibacy, availability - because the Church is family.
30. Charity - is the source, the means, and the end.
31. Christ adds value to our nothingness.
32. Christian: "greater is He who is in you than he who is in the world" (1John 4: 4).
33. Church crises? The gates of hell will not prevail (Matt. 16: 18).
34. Commitment of love.
35. Correct those who are confused (Júde 1: 22).
36. Daydreaming is not sensible.

37.   Different gifts, different ministries, different works – same Spirit, same Lord, same God (1Cor. 12: 4-6).

38.   Do all the good you can (cf. Gal. 6: 10).

39.   Do and disappear (Blessed Josemaria).

40.   Do everything possible and ask for what is impossible.

41.   Do everything with love (1Cor. 16: 14).

42.   Do good in good time.

43.   Do not be intimidated by your opponents (Phil. 1: 28).

44.   Do not delay baptism (John 3: 3, 5).

45.   Do not despise prophecies (2Thess. 5: 20).

46.   Do not grow lazy (Heb. 6: 12).

47.   Do not judge by appearances (Romans 2: 28).

48.   Do not labor for the food that perishes (John 6: 27).

49.   Do not prefer the praise of men to the glory of God (John 12: 43; cf. Romans 2: 29).

50.   Do not seek glory from men (1Thess. 2: 6).
51.   Do not stifle the spirit (2Thess. 5: 19).
52.   Do what you can, God will do the rest.
53.   Do whatever he tells you (John 2: 5).
54.   Do whatever you can while you can.
55.   Don't block your neighbour's way (Acts 5: 38-39; cf. Romans 14: 13).
56.   Don't keep the beggar begging (cf. Luke 6: 30).
57.   Don't preserve your life uselessly (Mark 8: 35; Luke 9: 24, 12: 4-5).
58.   Don't wait till you have surplus to give (Mark 12: 44).
59.   Dynamism! Don't get bored.
60.   Each one should be perfectly convinced she or he is understood.
61.   Each one should feel loved.
62.   Empathy more than sympathy (Heb. 13: 3).
63.   Every good gift and every perfect gift is from above,... from the Father of lights (James 1: 17).

64. Every moment is time for faith and time for reason.
65. Faith without works is as dead as a body without breath (James 2: 26).
66. Faithful in little things, faithful in much (cf. Matt. 25: 21; Luke 16: 10).
67. Fall in love.
68. Fan into flame, the gifts God has given (2Tim. 1: 6)
69. Fight!
70. For me to live is Christ (Phil. 1: 21).
71. For others: word, example and prayer, and the greatest of these is prayer.
72. For the things of God, holy shamelessness.
73. Force them to enter (cf. Luke 14: 23).
74. Forgive offenders (Luke 17: 4).
75. Friend of all.
76. Full measure (Luke 6: 38).
77. Give all - heart, body and soul.
78. Give and it shall be given unto you (Luke 6: 38).
79. Give to all who beg from you (Luke 6: 30).

80. Giving oneself means knowing oneself.
81. Go out and bear fruit.
82. Go to the byways and hedges.
83. God chastises dear ones (Rom.3: 19).
84. God is everywhere - follow Him.
85. God loves a cheerful giver (2 Cor. 9: 7).
86. God will repay every man for what he has done (Romans 2: 6, 10).
87. God's time is the best.
88. God's word is living and effective (Heb. 4: 12)
89. Great are the works of men and far greater are the works of he who made man.
90. Greater love has no man than this that he should lay down his life for his friends (John 15: 13).
91. Happy the man whose conscience does not condemn what he has chosen to do (Romans 14: 22-24).
92. Have no ambition except to do good.
93. Have supernatural outlook (John 3: 31).

94. Have the same mind as Jesus (Phil. 2: 5).
95. He wants none to perish but all to come to repentance (2Peter 3: 9).
96. He who loves his neighbor has fulfilled the law (Romans 13: 8, 10).
97. He wills that all men be saved (1 Tim. 2:4; cf. Acts 10: 28, 34).
98. Heal the world (pop song).
99. Help others to enjoy the blessings of God.
100. Heroism – of the mind, of the heart, of the flesh, of the spirit.
101. 'Holy man', be considerate (cf. Romans 15: 1).
102. Human leaders can only represent God, never displace nor replace God.
103. I am the servant of the Lord (Luke 1: 38).
104. I can do all things in Him who strengthens me (cf. Matt. 11: 28-30).
105. I glory in my ministry (Romans 11: 13).
106. If we are not faithful to God, we are not faithful to anything.

107.   In any and every way, let Christ be
        proclaimed (Phil. 1: 18).
108.   In days of peace, prepare for war.
109.   In His Church, God uses men, who
        may be weak, who may be unholy.
        (Acts 3: 12)
110.   In the apostolate, no delay.
111.   In the measure you give, you shall
        receive and more besides (Mark 4:
        24).
112.   It is good to help others persevere
        (3John 1: 6).
113.   It is better to give than to receive
        (Acts 20: 35).
114.   Join hands with those doing good.
115.   Justice: each one his name, each one
        his worth, each one his place, each
        one his way – as ordained by God
        (cf. Romans 13: 7).
116.   Keep peace of soul.
117.   Learn to do good (Isaiah 1: 16).
118.   Learn to labor and wait.
119.   Less lip service, more heart service
        (cf. Matt. 15: 8; Mark 7: 6; Psalm 78:
        36; Isaiah 29: 13).

120.   Less water, less wine (the miracle of Cana is the miracle of ordinary life) (cf. John 2: 1-11).
121.   Let him who would boast, boast in the Lord (2Cor. 10: 17).
122.   Let no stranger remain a stranger.
123.   Let us love in deed and truth (1John 3: 18).
124.   Let your light shine (Luke 8: 16, 11: 33).
125.   Let your money go round to all that need it.
126.   Live a life worthy of your calling (Eph. 1: 18, 4: 1).
127.   Live each day to the fullest.
128.   Live holy shamelessness.
129.   Love compels us to desire and care for the bodily and spiritual integrity of each person (cf. Sirach 30: 14-17).
130.   Love makes you act freely.
131.   Love never wrongs the neighbour (Romans 13: 10).
132.   Loyalty to lesser things should not impair loyalty to God.
133.   Make effort to improve things for the common good.

134.   Make even greater progress (1Thess. 4: 10).

135.   Make love your aim.

136.   Make progress and make other people progress (cf. 1Thess. 4: 1).

137.   Make sure your neighbor is happy.

138.   Many false prophets have appeared in the world (1John 4: 1).

139.   Many things are good, choose the more perfect, do the more perfect.

140.   Mine is to love and to suffer for Christ (cf. Phil. 1: 29).

141.   More intensity, more humility, more love.

142.   More, more, more.

143.   Multiply the fruits.

144.   Never say it's enough.

145.   No messenger outranks the one who sent him (John 13: 16).

146.   No hurry, no pause.

147.   No love but pure love.

148.   No man can serve two masters (Luke 16: 13).

149.   No pain, no gain (popular literature).

150.   No prophet is without honor except in his native place, among his own

kindred and in his own house (Matt. 13: 57; Mark 6: 4; Luke 4: 24; Acts 7: 52).

151. No pupil outranks his teacher, no slave his master (Matt. 10: 24; Luke 16: 13).

152. No true generosity without self-knowledge.

153. Not by sword (Matt. 26: 52).

154. Nothing done for God is ever wasted.

155. Nothing works well and nothing lasts without charity as its source, its means or its end.

156. Nothing superfluous should steal our time.

157. Offer everything to God.

158. One Lord, one faith, one baptism, one God (Eph. 4: 5).

159. One man sows; another reaps (John 4: 37).

160. Others first – sacrifice (Phil. 2: 4).

161. Our joy: Christ is being proclaimed (Phil. 1: 18).

162. Our knowledge is imperfect and our prophesying is imperfect. When the

perfect comes the imperfect will pass away (1Cor. 13: 10).

163. Pray: be attentive to prayer (Col. 4: 2-4).

164. Pray for understanding of the Scriptures (Luke 24: 45).

165. Pray that you may not be put to the test (Mark 14: 38; Luke 22: 40).

166. Prepare the way of the Lord, make straight His paths (Matt. 3: 3).

167. Progress always.

168. Proselytism is necessary.

169. Push things on with prayer.

170. Put your gifts at the service of one another, each in the measure he has received (1Peter 4: 10).

171. Rejoice with those who rejoice, weep with those who weep (Romans 12: 15).

172. Reliable in small things, reliable in great (cf. Matt. 25: 21).

173. *Relictis omnibus*. They left everything to follow Him (cf. Mark 10: 28).

174. Rely on the Holy Spirit (cf. Luke 12: 12; 21: 14-15; Acts 6: 10; Romans 8: 14-16, 26).
175. Remember the original Christian traditions (cf. 2Thess. 2: 15).
176. Rouse each other to love and good deeds (Heb. 10: 24).
177. Scandals will inevitably arise, but woe to him through whom they come (Luke 17: 1).
178. Seek the good of others (2Thess. 5: 15).
179. Self-discovery is the first step to self-giving.
180. Self-mastery (1Cor. 9: 27).
181. Self-esteem has meaning only in divine filiation.
182. Sing praise to the Lord with all your heart (Eph. 5: 19; Col. 3: 16).
183. Slave of all.
184. Solidarity - Christian solidarity - is Christian witness.
185. Some matters need only prayer (Mark 9: 29).
186. Some renounce sex for the sake of God's reign (Matt. 19: 12).

187. Some will be convinced; others will not believe (Acts 28: 24; Romans 10: 16).

188. Sow generously.

189. Special ones: children, sick, aged, and needy.

190. Special privilege: to suffer for Christ (cf. Phil. 1: 29).

191. Spend like the mother of a large and poor family - the Church.

192. Strive even more by good works to make your calling and election sure (2Peter 1: 10).

193. Strive for peace with all men (Heb. 12: 14).

194. Take care to discharge the ministry you have received in the Lord (Col. 4: 17).

195. Teachers will be called to the stricter account (James 3: 1).

196. Technology has increased the pleasures of this world but also the instruments of apostolate and good works.

197. The basic requirement: FAITH (cf. Gal. 2: 16, 3: 3-8; John 6: 29).

198.　The Church needs celibacy (Phil. 2: 17).

199.　The cross that is hard to bear is that of defending the truth.

200.　The crowds mean little, each soul means much.

201.　The duty of each moment should be in place.

202.　The fervent petition of a holy man is powerful indeed (James 5: 16).

203.　The gift you have received, give as a gift (Matt. 10: 8-9).

204.　The good shepherd lays down his life for his sheep (John 10: 11).

205.　The greatest…the one who serves the rest (Matt 23: 11; Mark 9: 35; Luke 22: 26).

206.　The harvest is great, the laborers few (Matt. 9: 37).

207.　The Holy Spirit is reward of obedience (Acts 5: 32).

208.　The Holy Spirit will move us to correct worship (1Cor. 12: 1-3).

209.　The Kingdom of God: a matter of justice, peace, and the joy that is given by the Holy Spirit (Romans 14: 17).

210. The Kingdom of God: to some in confidence, others by parables (cf. Matt. 13: 10-11; Mark 4: 11, 34).

211. The Kingdom of Heaven is at hand (Matt. 4: 17).

212. The laborers are few (Matt. 9: 37).

213. The love of Christ urges us on (2Cor. 5: 14).

214. The man who loves his life loses it (John 12: 25; cf. Matt. 16: 25).

215. The Master needs it. (Matt. 21: 3; Luke 19: 31; Mark 11: 3).

216. The more ambitious you are, the more patience you need.

217. The more wickedness we see the more we must pray.

218. The most generous are the least known for it.

219. The most useful people are the free and happy.

220. The Pauline armor for spiritual warfare: truth, justice, zeal for the Gospel, faith, Word of God (cf. Eph. 6: 14-17).

221.   The pen is mightier than the sword (popular literature).

222.   The poor you will always have with you (Mark 14: 7; John 12: 8).

223.   The price of Heaven - give yourself.

224.   The saints will shine like the sun in their Father's Kingdom (Matt. 13: 43).

225.   The salvation of souls is in your hands.

226.   The shepherd who does not pray is not safe (John 10: 9).

227.   The signs of good health, the signs of youth are compatible with celibacy.

228.   The spiritual man can appraise everything (1Cor. 2: 15).

229.   The standards of holiness cannot be lowered.

230.   The teacher must be preoccupied learning.

231.   The wisdom of love knows how.

232.   The Word of God is the helmet of salvation and the sword of the spirit (Eph. 6: 17).

233.   There are souls waiting (Romans 10: 14-15).

234.   There are things God wants from me (Luke 19: 29).
235.   There is a season for everything (Eccl. 3: 1).
236.   There is much to be done.
237.   There is no authority except from God (Romans 13: 1).
238.   There is only one true Christianity with no left wings and no right wings (cf. 1Cor 1: 10-13, 12-14; 11: 19).
239.   There shall be one flock, one shepherd (John 10: 16).
240.   Thin sowing, thin reaping (cf. 2Cor. 9: 6).
241.   Things take time so start in time.
242.   Things that are *"corban"* may become sins of omission (Matt. 15: 5-6).
243.   Think globally, act locally (WHO slogan).
244.   This is the work of God: have faith in the One whom he sent (John 6: 29).
245.   Those who live according to the flesh are intent on the things of the flesh and those who live according to

the spirit, on those of the spirit
(Romans 8: 5).

246. Those who rely on God are dynamic.

247. Through Him, with Him, in Him - to
the end (cf. Phil 1: 6).

248. To Caesar what is Caesar's…to God
what is God's (cf. Matt. 22: 21;
Mark 12: 17; Luke 20: 25).

249. To serve be useful (Blessed
Josemaria).

250. To whom much is given, much is
required (Luke 12: 48).

251. Train yourself for the life of piety
(1Tim. 4: 7).

252. Treat others as you would like them
to treat you (Matt. 7: 12).

253. Trials are our common lot (1Thess.
3: 3).

254. True generosity is universal.

255. True unity derives from the Holy
Spirit and is characterized by peace
(cf. Eph. 4: 3-6).

256. Unenlightened zeal is not justified
(Romans 10: 12).

257. United we stand, divided we fall
(popular literature).

258.   Unity in variety (Romans 12: 4).
259.   Value each person.
260.   Value the things that really matter (Phil. 1: 10).
261.   Volunteer.
262.   Watch yourself and watch your teaching (1Tim. 4: 16).
263.   Watchful love.
264.   We are ambassadors for Christ (2Cor. 5: 20).
265.   We are children of God - in times of war, in times of peace - we are children of God.
266.   We cannot but speak of what we have seen and heard (Acts 4: 20).
267.   We cannot improve anything without effort.
268.   We have only one Christianity which many live *in part* and few *in whole.*
269.   We have to work for God, with God, immersed in God.
270.   We must be content but not satisfied for there is much to be done.
271.   We must grow in knowledge of God and His will (Eph. 1: 17-18; Col. 1: 9-10).

272.　We must lay down our lives for our brothers (1John 3: 16).

273.　We must show filiation to the clergy (Acts 2: 42, 16: 4; 1Cor. 10: 33).

274.　We must wash each other's feet (John 13: 14).

275.　We must yield fruit as God wants not as we want (Mark 11: 13-14; Luke 19: 26).

276.　We reap as we sow (cf. 2Cor. 9: 6).

277.　We shall overcome (Martin Luther King Jr.).

278.　We should ask God for vocations (cf. Luke 10: 12).

279.　We should glory in the Cross of Our Lord Jesus Christ (cf. Gal. 6: 14).

280.　We walk by faith (2Cor. 5: 7).

281.　Wealth is for administration not accumulation (1Tim. 6: 17-19; cf. 2Cor. 8: 15).

282.　What does it profit a man to gain the whole world and destroy himself in the process? (Matt. 16: 26; Mark 8: 36; Luke 9: 25).

283.　What matters is keeping God's commandments (1Cor. 7: 19).

284.   What you have is for the Common
        Good (cf. 1Cor. 12: 7).
285.   What you hear in private proclaim
        from the housetops (Matt. 10: 27).
286.   Whatever you do, do in the name of
        the Lord Jesus (Col. 3: 17).
287.   When the going gets tough, the
        tough get going (popular literature).
288.   When there is love, we are not
        limited by time or space or means;
        love over-rules them.
289.   Who will separate us from the love
        of Christ? (Romans 8: 35).
290.   Whoever loves God must also love
        his brother (1John 4: 21).
291.   Whoever wants to rank first… must
        serve the needs of all (Matt. 20: 27;
        Mark 10: 44).
292.   Wise men still seek Jesus.
293.   With God all things are possible
        (Mark 10: 27; Luke 1: 37).
294.   With God: sooner, more and better
        (Blessed Josemaria).
295.   Without faith, it is impossible to
        please God (Heb. 11: 6).

296. Without the Scriptures we are not fully equipped for good works (2Tim. 3: 16-17).

297. Work for the salvation of all.

298. Work? Cheerfully (cf. Romans 12: 8).

299. You are a "chosen race, a royal priesthood, a holy nation…" (1Peter 2: 9).

300. You are the salt of the earth but what if salt goes flat (Matt. 5: 13; Luke 14: 34).

301. You are your first student (cf. Romans 2: 21-24).

302. You can tell a tree by its fruit (Matt. 12: 33).

303. You must esteem the person of every man (1Peter 2: 17).

304. You must keep converting yourself and others.

305. You will receive all that you pray for provided you have faith (Matt. 21: 22).

306. You will suffer in the world (John 16: 33).

307.   Your light *must* shine before men
        (Matt. 5: 16).
308.   Your relief of others ought not to
        impoverish you (2Cor. 8: 12-13).
309.   Your widow's mite is your
        everything (Luke 21: 4).

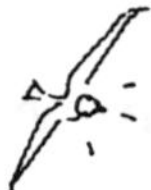 ## *SECTION IV*
SPIRITUAL JOLTS 

1. A household split into fractions cannot last for long (cf. Matt. 12: 25; Luke 11: 17).
2. A sanctified memory is the memory of God.
3. Acknowledge your sins (1Peter 1: 9).
4. Always be free but not to sin (cf. 1Peter 2: 16).
5. Apologize.
6. Ask for a delicate conscience.
7. At all times - vigilance.
8. Avoid envies (cf. James 3: 16, 4: 1-10; 1Peter 2: 16).
9. Avoid people who do evil (2Tim. 3: 25).
10. Be busy but not a busybody (cf. 2Thess. 3: 11).
11. Be careful not to parade your good deeds (Matt. 6: 1).
12. Be extra watchful in sickness and tiredness.

13.   Be on the look out against hypocritical teaching (cf. Matt. 16: 6; Luke 12: 1).
14.   Be on your guard against idols (1John 5: 21).
15.   Be on your guard constantly (Mark 13: 5, 9, 28, 37).
16.   Be prepared.
17.   Be quick to hear, slow to speak (James 1: 19).
18.   Bear with one another lovingly (Eph. 4: 2; cf. Gal. 6: 2).
19.   Believe in the Way of the Cross.
20.   Beware of confusion and deception (cf. 2Cor. 11: 4; Gal. 1: 7-9, 5: 7-10; Eph. 4: 14; Phil. 3: 2; Colossians 2: 8; 2 Thess. 3: 2).
21.   Beware of empty reverence (Matt. 15: 9).
22.   Beware of false doctrines (1Tim. 1: 2; 1Tim. 4: 1-5).
23.   Beware of money, sensuality and power.
24.   Beware of pleasures which cloud the mind and distort judgement.
25.   Beware of short cuts.

26.   Beware of unconscious egoism.
27.   But beware of men (Matt. 10: 17).
28.   By your words you will be acquitted, and by your words you will be condemned (Matthew 12: 37; Romans 2: 1).
29.   Cease to do evil (Isaiah 1: 16).
30.   Consider how you have fared (Haggai 1: 1-8).
31.   Constant reliance on grace.
32.   Constant self-examination.
33.   Corruption of the best is the worst (popular literature).
34.   Daily conversions of self.
35.   Do examination of conscience conscientiously.
36.   Do good and avoid evil (Romans 12: 9).
37.   Do not ... let sin rule over your mortal body (Roman 6: 12).
38.   Do not approve others' sins (Romans 2: 32).
39.   Do not be wise in your own estimation (Romans 12: 16).
40.   Do not condemn (Luke 7: 37).

41.   Do not continue in ignorance….but
      discern God's will (cf. Eph. 5: 17).
42.   Do not dance with danger.
43.   Do not give the devil a chance to
      work on you (Eph. 4: 27).
44.   Do not imitate what is evil but what
      is good (3John 1: 11).
45.   Do not judge (Luke 7: 37).
46.   Do not judge by appearances (cf.
      Romans 2: 28).
47.   Do not look at what is not licit to
      desire (cf. 1Cor. 10: 6).
48.   Do not love money (Heb. 13: 5).
49.   Do not lust after evil things. (1 Cor.
      9: 6)
50.   Do not return evil for evil or insult
      for insult (1Peter 3: 9).
51.   Do not trust the malicious (cf. Sirach
      37: 10-15).
52.   Do not welcome evil doctrine (2John
      1:10-11).
53.   Do violence to your weaknesses.
54.   Don't be a saint alone.
55.   Don't be an enemy of the Cross of
      Christ (cf. Phil. 3: 18).
56.   Don't be deaf (Mark 4: 9).

57.   Don't co-operate with evil.
58.   Don't lie to yourself.
59.   Don't set the stage for trouble.
60.   Don't set yourself as a model
        without God.
61.   Don't take virtues for granted.
62.   Don't tempt your neighbor.
63.   Don't waste.
64.   Envy blinds (cf. Acts 5: 17, 7: 9;
        Mark 9: 39, 10: 47, 50).
65.   Envy is always unnecessary.
66.   Even Satan disguises himself as an
        angel of light (2Cor. 11: 14).
67.   Every planting not by God will be
        uprooted (cf. Matt. 15: 13).
68.   Everyone who exalts himself shall be
        humbled (Luke 18: 14).
69.   Examine your heart frequently (cf.
        2Cor. 13: 5; Gal. 6: 4).
70.   Exercise authority with care (cf.
        Rom. 12: 8).
71.   Faithful today, faithful tomorrow.
72.   Fear ignorance.
73.   Fear to do your will.
74.   Flee from the worship of idols. (1
        Cor. 10: 4)

75.   Follow good example (Phil. 3: 17); 1Thess. 1: 6).

76.   Forget Egypt (cf. Exodus 16: 2-3; 17: 3, 7).

77.   Freedom: human precepts can never be dogmas (cf. Matt. 15: 9; Mark 7: 7).

78.   Frequent the Sacraments.

79.   From dust to dust (Gen. 2: 7; Eccl. 12: 7).

80.   Fun? Don't get carried away (Luke 21: 34).

81.   Get to know yourself.

82.   Give some evidence that you mean to reform (Luke 3: 80).

83.   Give way to what is good and true.

84.   Go first to be reconciled with your brother (Matt. 5: 37).

85.   Go to the roots.

86.   God does not test us beyond our strength (1Cor. 10: 13).

87.   God is kind so that we may repent (Romans 2: 4).

88.   God reads our hearts (Acts 15: 8).

89.   God resists the proud: gives grace to the humble (James 4: 6).

90. God will help the sinner not the self-righteous (Mark 2: 17; Luke 5: 32).
91. Good people are not good enough without God.
92. Grumbling is not worthwhile (cf. 1Cor. 10: 10).
93. Harden not your heart (Roman 2: 5; Hebrews 3: 8).
94. Have a habit of self-examination.
95. He must increase; I must decrease (John 3: 30).
96. He who seeks only himself brings himself to ruin (Matt. 10: 39).
97. If you are angry – let it be without sin (Eph. 4: 26).
98. In busy times, pray earlier not later.
99. In pious practices – serenity.
100. Interest - not curiosity.
101. Judgement comes (James 2: 12).
102. Keep an eye on the enemy.
103. Keep an eye on tomorrow.
104. Keep salt in your heart and you will be at peace with one another (Mark 9: 50).
105. Know your manias.

106.   Less lip service, more heart service (cf. Matt. 15: 8; Mark 7: 6; Luke 12: 47).
107.   Let every one heed what he hears (Matt. 13: 9, 43; Luke 11: 28).
108.   Let everyone obey the authorities that are over him (Romans 13: 1).
109.   Let him who would boast, boast in the Lord (1Cor. 1: 31).
110.   Let no man separate what God has joined (Matt. 19: 6; Mark 10: 9).
111.   Let no one deceive you (Matt. 24: 4; Romans 1: 32; Luke 12: 1).
112.   Let no one mislead you (Mark 13: 5).
113.   Let the marriage bed be undefiled. (Heb. 13: 4)
114.   Lukewarmness is a sickness of the will.
115.   Lukewarmness is disgusting (Rev. 3: 16).
116.   Maintain the sense of sin.
117.   Make haste slowly (popular literature).
118.   Mortify your members (Col. 3: 5).
119.   Never get used to anything: Love!
120.   Never indifference.

121. Never lay hands hastily on anyone (1Tim. 5: 22).
122. Never take it easy unnecessarily.
123. New wine is poured into new wineskins (Matt. 2: 22).
124. No idle moments, even at rest.
125. No resistance to grace or God's work.
126. None is immune from sin, error and ignorance.
127. None of us lives as his own master, and none of us dies as his own master.... we are the Lord's (Romans 14: 7-8).
128. Nothing is anything and everything is nothing without charity.
129. Now is the acceptable time (2Cor. 6: 2).
130. Obedience to God is the best sacrifice (1Sam. 15: 22).
131. Often, we can only pray and do nothing (cf. Mark 9: 29).
132. Oil your lamp in good time (cf. Matt. 25: 1-13).
133. Old sins come back in new forms.

134. One who has no love for the brother he has seen cannot love God he has not seen (1John 4: 20).

135. Only one thing is necessary – LOVE (Luke 10: 41; Romans 13: 8-10).

136. Passion blinds.

137. Passions are buried alive - hibernating, waiting for their season.

138. Pay each one his dues (Romans 13: 7).

139. People who look for God for their own good may fail to become good.

140. Perfect contrition means avoiding sin.

141. Perfect love means keeping his commandments (1John 2: 5).

142. Pleasure can lead to displeasure.

143. Pray that you may not undergo the test (Matt. 26: 41; Mark 14: 38; Luke 21: 36; Luke 22: 40).

144. Pray without ceasing (cf. Eph. 6: 18).

145. Pride disturbs the work of grace.

146. Pride goes before a fall (popular literature)

147. Put aside your old self with its past deeds (Col. 3: 9).

148. Put on a new man – anew in the image of the creator (cf. Col. 3: 9-11).
149. Rectitude of intention.
150. Resist the devil and he will take flight (James 4: 7; 1Peter 5: 9).
151. Sacrifice the fallen nature – live the new life (cf. Romans 6: 3-11; 8: 8-12).
152. Satan disguises as an angel of light (cf. 2Cor. 11:14).
153. Search for justice (Isaiah 1: 17).
154. Seek first the Kingdom of God (cf. Matt. 6: 33; Luke 12: 31).
155. Seek the things that are above (Col. 3: 1).
156. Self control.
157. Self-estimation should be sober (Romans 12: 13).
158. Sin has such power to complicate us (cf. John 8: 31-47).
159. Sincere love (Romans 12: 9).
160. Speak the truth (Eph. 4: 25).
161. The day of the Lord is coming like a thief in the night (1Thess 5: 2).

162. The devil tries to destroy our courage.

163. The devil would make us worship anything other than God.

164. The dog returns to its vomit (2Peter 2: 22).

165. The fear of the Lord is the beginning of wisdom (Sirach 1:16; Psalm 111:10)

166. The greatest mediocrity is sin.

167. The love of money is the root of all evil. (Tim 6: 2-12).

168. The man who does not love is among the living dead (1John 3: 14).

169. The most captivating idol - self.

170. The one who prays will never miss his road.

171. The sensual man does not perceive the things that are of the Spirit of God (1Cor. 2: 14).

172. The tongue is such a flame (James 3: 6).

173. There are obstacles inside and outside.

174.   There is no limit to what envy can do (cf. Matt. 27: 18; Mark 15: 10; Acts 7: 9; Acts 13: 45).

175.   There is only one Christianity, to be lived in whole and not in part.

176.   Those who look for faults find them.

177.   Today Hosanna! Tomorrow Crucify Him!

178.   Try to lose nothing of what God has given you (John 6: 39).

179.   Unless we are humble we will not know peace.

180.   Unless we understand the value of the scriptures and grace, we are badly misled (cf. Matt 21: 29).

181.   Vice - beware of time-robbing vice.

182.   Virile but virtuous.

183.   Watch (cf. Matt. 25: 13; Mark 13: 37).

184.   Watch you tongue (cf. Eph. 4: 29).

185.   Watch yourself (1Cor. 10: 12; Eph. 5: 15).

186.   Wear an invisible cloak of prayer and atonement.

187.   What began in the spirit can end in the flesh (cf. Gal. 3: 3).

188. What have you that you have not received? (1Cor. 4:7).
189. Whatever causes sin, cut it off (Matt. 18: 8-9).
190. When the body is well the soul dances (St. Augustine of Hippo).
191. Who am I that I should interfere with what God is doing for others? (cf. Acts 11: 18).
192. Who are you to judge your neighbour? (James 4: 12).
193. Who is like God?
194. Who loves danger will perish in it (Sirach 3: 27).
195. Whoever exalts himself will be humbled (Matt. 23: 12; Luke 18: 14).
196. Work for your salvation in anxious fear (Phil 2: 12).
197. Worship God alone (Rev. 18: 10; 22: 8-9).
198. You do not know what will happen tomorrow (James 4: 14).
199. You err because you know neither the Scriptures nor the power of God (Matt. 22: 29).
200. You have no right to persist in sin.

201. You have spent too much time doing
      what the pagans do (cf. 1Peter 4:3).
202. You have to leave sin.
203. You shall do homage to the Lord
      your God. Him alone shall you adore
      (Matt. 4: 10; Luke 4: 8; Rev. 22: 9).

THINGS TO TREASURE

Many times we fall into error or wrong habits or we fall short of good ones because we are neglecting some good which we should involve ourselves with more. Below are a list of some treasures, ideas and ideals that are often overlooked by ourselves and our contemporaries. We could meditate on these matters as they relate to our lives: how we value them, promote them, and take advantage of them. We could pray about them frequently and ask for advice in spiritual direction concerning them.

1. The Supreme Good – God.
2. His Name, His Will, His Kingdom.
3. Grace.
4. Love.
5. Interior sensitivity.
6. Silence.
7. The Paraclete.
8. Divine Filiation.
9. Holy Communion.
10. Time.
11. Other people.
12. Refinement of conscience.
13. Justice.

14.   Harmony.
15.   Goodwill.
16.   Freedom.
17.   Truth.
18.   Joy.
19.   Discipline.
20.   Discretion.
21.   Foresight.
22.   Sincerity.
23.   Talents.
24.   Common good.
25.   Providence.
26.   Vision.
27.   Friendship.
28.   Politics.
29.   Music.
30.   Effort.
31.   Rest.
32.   Intuition.
33.   Youth.
34.   Diplomacy.
35.   Art.
36.   Perception.
37.   Fraternity.
38.   Equality.
39.   Inspiration.

40. Patriotism.
41. Study.
42. Advice.
43. Constancy.
44. Repentance.
45. The Cross.
46. Human dignity.
47. Little things.
48. Correction.
49. Insight.
50. Culture.
51. Sports.
52. Progress.
53. Education.
54. Health.
55. Christian formation.
56. Death.

DANGERS

The human nature, we all know, is essentially wounded by original sin but restored by the grace of God through Jesus Christ in Baptism and other sacraments. This restoration is however generally not kept intact because of further sin and therefore comes to depend on our progressive re-union with Jesus Christ. There are obstacles in the way. Firstly and above all, the devil who "goes around like a roaring lion seeking for someone to devour" (1Peter 5: 8) and secondly our pride (over-estimation of self; conceit) which, as Blessed Josemaria liked to put it, dies twenty-four hours after its owner. Pride is often deep and steady and through it we can walk into many dangers which can so rule us that they affect our interior life of grace. Some of these dangers are listed below for our frequent examination, resolution, prayer and struggle.

1.   Satan.
2.   Hardness of heart.
3.   Self love.
4.   The flesh.
5.   Despair.
6.   Hatred.
7.   Wealth.

8.   Pleasure.
9.   Success.
10.   Fanaticism (Matt. 4: 10).
11.   Sentimentality.
12.   Curiosity.
13.   Anxiety (Matt. 6: 25-34).
14.   Power.
15.   Routine (Matt. 5: 20).
16.   Lukewarmness (Luke 14: 34-35).
17.   Flattery.
18.   Rebellion.
19.   Comparisons.
20.   Bitterness.
21.   Excuses.
22.   Cowardice.
23.   Mediocrity.
24.   Compensations.
25.   Hypocrisy (Matt. 7: 1-5).
26.   Ambition.
27.   Vanity.
28.   Arrogance.
29.   Destructive criticism (Matt. 7: 1-5).
30.   Malice.
31.   Whims.
32.   Complications.
33.   Fear.

34.   Forgetfulness.
35.   Prejudice.
36.   Meanness
37.   Insincerity.
38.   Frivolity.
39.   Complicity.
40.   Aversion.
41.   Presumption (Matt. 8: 12).
42.   False prophets (Matt. 7: 15).
43.   Disorder.
44.   Easy life.

ASPIRATIONS

Aspirations, ejaculations, and spiritual communions are short prayers raised sporadically to God in our hearts throughout the day. They are typical of souls who have God in mind and so spontaneously refer to Him. Such prayers, because they are short, simple and spontaneous, are possible at all times in all circumstances and will come to us easily at the moment of our death if we are in the habit of praying them.

Sometimes we are mindful of the presence of God in our lives but fall short of words. It may help us to use the words of other people that may have left some impression on us. There are many words of Jesus in the Gospel that can serve this purpose. In fact, Jesus by His example has taught us to pray ejaculations: "I bless you Father, Lord of Heaven and earth for revealing these truths to mere children" (Matt. 11:25); "Father, into your hands I commend my spirit" (Luke 23:46).

The Apostles' and disciples' words and those of simple peasants in the Gospel are also very useful aspirations that we can repeat time and again: "Lord, teach us to pray" (Luke 11:1); "Lord, show us the Father" (John 14:8); "O Lord, be merciful to me a sinner" (Luke 18:13); "Lord, it is good for us to be here" (Matt. 17:4; Mark 9: 4; Luke 9: 33). We may also like to use words from the Psalms or the Book of Wisdom:

"Lord, in the secret of my heart teach me wisdom" (Psalm 51: 8); or words of saints throughout time: "Late have I loved you!" (St. Augustine of Hippo) or simply words that come to us when we pray or read or work which we somehow retain and thus repeat regularly to keep united to God. The following are a brief collection. They may be useful in many instances, for example:

-when our prayer is dry and lifeless
-when it seems we do not have time to pray
-while we do our work
-while we walk down a corridor, while waiting or on a journey
-as aids to talk to Jesus after receiving Holy Communion
-in between activities or events of each day.

These simple prayers - help us to use our time well. A single sentence could be a focus for some five - ten minutes meditation. A single sentence could also be something we stick to our mind to carry around for a whole day.

It is better to avoid reading continually without pausing or reflecting as that is not the purpose of this chapter. The aim is to provide words to inspire prayer when it is difficult and not to supply reading material.

 ## SECTION I
FAITH 

1. Father, help me to keep my baptismal vows all the days of my life.
2. Father help me to do everything for your glory.
3. Father, you have the power to do all things.
4. God knows best.
5. How good God is.
6. I can do all things in him who strengthens me (Phil. 4:13).
7. I count it a supreme advantage to know Christ Jesus (cf. Phil. 3: 8).
8. I know that my redeemer lives (Job 19: 25).
9. I know whom I have loved.
10. I'm sure you will not abandon me.
11. It is the Lord! (John 21: 7).
12. Jesus, make sure I follow you closely.
13. Lord, fill us with faith.

14.   Lord, help me believe all that you have said.

15.   Lord, help me to live as you want me to live.

16.   Lord, help me to show the world what grace can do.

17.   Lord, help my lack of trust (Mark 9: 24).

18.   Lord, help us fulfil your will, always and everywhere.

19.   Lord, help us to believe that we need you.

20.   Lord, help us to proclaim our faith by all that we say and do.

21.   Lord, help us to receive you and all that comes from you - most solemnly.

22.   Lord, I believe in you.

23.   Lord, I cling to you for salvation.

24.   Lord, I firmly believe you are with me.

25.   Lord, I hope in you.

26.   Lord, I will never disown you (Matt. 26:35).

27.   Lord, I'm in search of greatness.

28.   Lord, keep me within your true
        Church - the catholic.
29.   Lord, let me never fear death.
30.   Lord, make me a believer.
31.   Lord, make me act with the power of
        wisdom.
32.   Lord, make me call you Father.
33.   Lord, make me draw good from each
        situation.
34.   Lord, make me ever more sensitive
        to your grace.
35.   Lord, make me have faith in you and
        in all that comes from you and in all
        that leads to you.
36.   Lord, make me live a life of faith.
37.   Lord, make me open with my faith;
        clear and militant with my faith.
38.   Lord, show me time for faith and
        time for reason.
39.   Lord, show that I'm working for you.
40.   Lord, help me - that I may see.
41.   Lord, to whom shall we go? You
        have the message of Eternal Life
        (John 6: 68).
42.   Lord, we can! (Matt. 20: 22; Mark
        10: 39).

43.   My God, I believe that all that is
       yours is mine (cf. Luke 15: 31).
44.   Not my will, but Thine be done
       (Matt. 26: 39; Mark 14: 36; Luke 22:
       42).
45.   *Omnia in bonum* - All for good (cf.
       Romans 8: 28).

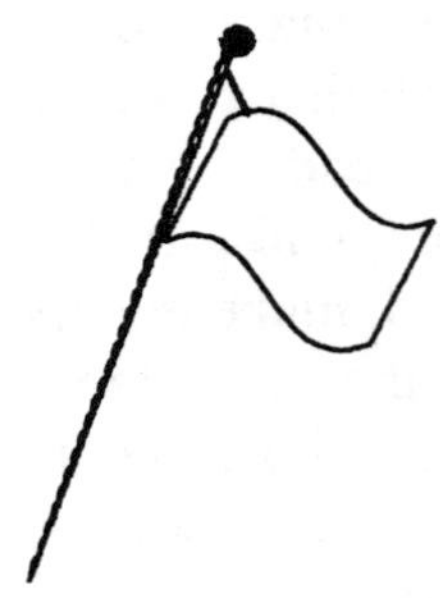

SECTION II
WORSHIP

1. Blessed be God!
2. Father, Lord of Heaven and earth, to you I offer praise (Matt. 11: 25).
3. Father, my Father! (cf. Mark 14: 36; Galatians 4: 6; Romans 8: 16)
4. I bless you Father, Lord of heaven and earth (cf. Matt. 11: 25)
5. Jesus, show that you are Lord!
6. Lord you alone are the Holy One (cf. Matt. 19: 17; Mark 10: 18; Luke 18: 19).
7. Lord, I thank you for the wonder of my being (cf. Psalm 139: 14).
8. Lord, make sure that I love you, make sure I worship you, make sure I obey you.
9. Lord, show that you are Master.
10. Lord, yours is the Kingdom, the power and the glory (Liturgy).
11. Master of history, Lord of life!
12. Master! (Luke 5: 5; 8: 24).
13. My Lord and my God! (John 20: 28).

14. O God, our refuge and our strength.
15. *Omnipotens Sempiterne Deus!!*
     (Blessed Josemaria).
16. Reign Master Jesus!

SECTION III
SUPERNATURAL LOVE

1. Be with me Lord, help me to be with you.
2. Father, give us brotherly love.
3. How I love you, Jesus.
4. I just want to love you, Jesus.
5. I will lay down my life for you John 13: 37).
6. I'm for your pleasure, Lord!
7. Jesus, give me the power to suffer when others suffer.
8. Jesus, give me your Spirit, make me a child of God in earnest.
9. Lord, as you do for me - full measure, pressed down and flowing over - so let me do for you (cf. Luke 6: 38).
10. Lord, be at home in me.
11. Lord, direct my feet to Heaven.
12. Lord, engrave in me your New Covenant, that law of love, of grace, of freedom, that law of your gospel.
13. Lord, give me a heart for all.

14. Lord, give me fervor for prayer, fervor for ~~apostate~~ apostolate, fervor for work.
15. Lord, give me grace for all, time for all, and the means for all.
16. Lord, give me knowledge, that leads to understanding, that leads to love.
17. Lord, give me order in my mind, order in my heart, order in my intellect and order in my will.
18. Lord, give me the order of charity and give me that order with clarity.
19. Lord, give me the vigilance of love.
20. Lord, give us catholic hearts.
21. Lord, help me care for whatever pleases you.
22. Lord, help me not to think badly about anyone and not to think well about myself.
23. Lord, help me to appreciate your love.
24. Lord, help me to choose what is most pleasing to you.
25. Lord, help me to do you proud always.
26. Lord, help me to enjoy the enjoyment of others.

27.   Lord, help me to leave behind all the good I can.

28.   Lord, help me to love you genuinely.

29.   Lord, help me to love you tremendously.

30.   Lord, help me to love you with deeds.

31.   Lord, help me to please you.

32.   Lord, help me to talk to you.

33.   Lord, help me to want all that you want of me.

34.   Lord, help us to correct each other charitably.

35.   Lord, help us to recognize you at the breaking of the bread (cf. Luke 24: 35).

36.   Lord, I give you my heart, the whole and not a part.

37.   Lord, I love everything that you do.

38.   Lord, I love you.

39.   Lord, I want nothing for myself, all for you.

40.   Lord, I want to be your friend, teach me everything (cf. John 15: 15).

41.   Lord, I want to do good.

42.   Lord, I want to have you as my theme.
43.   Lord, I want to love you in the fullness of my being.
44.   Lord, I want to love you with all of me.
45.   Lord, I want to please you in all things.
46.   Lord, I want to see your face (cf. Psalm 42: 3).
47.   Lord, I want you.
48.   Lord, I will give you all I can.
49.   Lord, I will not wait for old age to have time for you.
50.   Lord, I'd rather disappoint me than to disappoint you.
51.   Lord, I'm ambitious for love - guide my zeal.
52.   Lord, I'm only human but always remember I love you.
53.   Lord, I'm so in love with you.
54.   Lord, increase my capacity to do good.
55.   Lord, increase my capacity to pray.
56.   Lord, increase my desire to do good.

57.   Lord, it is good for us to be with you (cf. Matt. 17: 4).
58.   Lord, keep bringing my attention to you.
59.   Lord, keep from me a malicious spirit.
60.   Lord, let it be that only your Spirit subdues me.
61.   Lord, let me be always where I am needed.
62.   Lord, let me do no evil; speak no evil; think no evil.
63.   Lord, let me love you, in my flesh, in my heart, in my mind, in my will.
64.   Lord, let me please you with little things, with great things, with everything.
65.   Lord, let me teach love in all I say and do.
66.   Lord, let our hearts burn within us as we spend this time with you (cf. Luke 24: 32).
67.   Lord, LOVE! Engrave this law in me.
68.   Lord, make charity and wisdom direct my struggle.

69.   Lord, make me 100% yours.
70.   Lord, make me a monstrance of charity.
71.   Lord, make me aware of the needs of people.
72.   Lord, make me forgive like you do.
73.   Lord, make me free to do what love compels me to do.
74.   Lord, make me fruitful by your love.
75.   Lord, make me fulfil my mission generously.
76.   Lord, make me give all I've gained.
77.   Lord, make me grasp well the mentality of each person.
78.   Lord, make me leave a legacy of love.
79.   Lord, make me live for you alone.
80.   Lord, make me live up to your expectation.
81.   Lord, make me love the Holy Mass.
82.   Lord, make me love you above sin.
83.   Lord, make me love you with deeds and above deeds - make me just love you.
84.   Lord, make me mature in love.
85.   Lord, make me merciful.

86.   Lord, make me quick in giving what
        I can give.
87.   Lord, make me really good.
88.   Lord, make me see in people what
        you see in them.
89.   Lord, make me sensitive to the
        dictates of love.
90.   Lord, make me sow love, make me
        sow peace, make me sow joy, make
        me sow unity, make me sow
        progress.
91.   Lord, make me take others seriously.
92.   Lord, make me treat my body with
        piety.
93.   Lord, make me truly poor, truly
        detached from all else and truly rich
        before you.
94.   Lord, make us know you; make us
        happy.
95.   Lord, may I always inspire goodness.
96.   Lord, may I never forget the poor
        (cf. Galatians 2: 10).
97.   Lord, may I never forget the sinner.
98.   Lord, may I never forget you.
99.   Lord, may I never grow less in love.

100. Lord, may my love for you be fruitful.
101. Lord, may my works extend your love and mercy to others.
102. Lord, may we have friends indeed (cf. Luke 22: 28).
103. Lord, open my eyes to all the good I can do.
104. Lord, stay with us! (Luke 24: 29).
105. Lord, teach me how to please you.
106. Lord, teach me to save others from envy.
107. Lord, teach me who my neighbor is (cf. Luke 10: 27, 29).
108. Lord, you are so easy to forget - help me to stop forgetting you.
109. Loving Father!
110. Make me love you till the end.
111. Lord, strengthen my will to do your will.

 # SECTION IV
THANKSGIVING 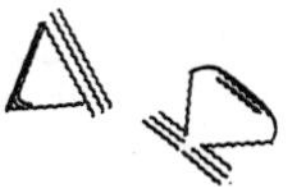

1. Father, I thank you for having heard me (John 11: 41).
2. Lord, help me to give you thanks – truly, always and everywhere.
3. Lord, how good of you to even promise us things.
4. Lord, make me appreciate the beauty of your gospel.
5. Lord, make me appreciate the redemption.
6. Lord, make me rejoice in you.
7. Lord, thank you for your availability in the Holy Eucharist.
8. Lord, thank you for your sacraments.
9. Lord, thank you.
10. Lord, thank you for the wonder of my being (cf. psalm 139: 14).

 **SECTION V
REPARATION** 

1.   Blessed be pain (Blessed Josemaria).
2.   Can't serve two masters (Matt. 6: 24; Luke 16: 13).
3.   Get behind me Satan! (Matt. 16: 23).
4.   I glory in my infirmity. When I am weak then I am strong.
5.   Jesus, may I sin less and less each day.
6.   Late have I loved you! (Saint Augustine of Hippo).
7.   Lord, give us simplicity and Godly sincerity (cf. 2Cor. 1: 12).
8.   Lord, help me to make up to you for all the idolatry around.
9.   Lord, bless and approve my sufferings for you.
10. Lord, call me to conversion constantly.
11. Lord, continue to restore our lives.
12. Lord, deliver us from confused and evil men (cf. 2Thess. 3: 2).

13. Lord, do not remember the sins of my youth.
14. Lord, give me courage to resist temptations.
15. Lord, give me holy purity now.
16. Lord, give me sorrow of love.
17. Lord, grant us the peace of the way of the Cross.
18. Lord, help me not to disappoint you.
19. Lord, help me root out my defects as soon as possible.
20. Lord, help me to know what offends you.
21. Lord, help me to prefer to avoid sin than to do penance for my sins.
22. Lord, help me to react to lukewarmness.
23. Lord, help me to remember there are too many sins and I should not add to them.
24. Lord, help me to resolve firmly not to sin again.
25. Lord, help me to suffer to please you.
26. Lord, help us defeat the power of sin and evil.

27. Lord, help us desire your mercy.
28. Lord, help us reverse what scandal has done.
29. Lord, I am sorry I am still capable of sin.
30. Lord, I offer you the frustrations of the flesh.
31. Lord, I want to be merciful as you are merciful.
32. Lord, I want to die like you did.
33. Lord, I will fight!
34. Lord, I'd rather die that to sin but I sin.
35. Lord, I'm terribly short of love.
36. Lord, keep me faithful in spite of everything.
37. Lord, keep me from sin.
38. Lord, keep me safe from ignorance, sin and error: mine and those of others.
39. Lord, let me be slow to condemn.
40. Lord, look not on our sin
41. Lord, make me avoid occasions of sin.
42. Lord, make me aware of my weaknesses.

43.   Lord, make me careful in avoiding disorder.

44.   Lord, make me concerned that you are not offended.

45.   Lord, make me constant in conversion.

46.   Lord, make me courageous in examining myself.

47.   Lord, make me fight violently against all my sins.

48.   Lord, make me less a sinner each day.

49.   Lord, make me more useful to you.

50.   Lord, make me recognize each and every temptation.

51.   Lord, make me redeem the time I've wasted.

52.   Lord, make me resolve firmly not to sin again.

53.   Lord, make me see the source of my sin and flee.

54.   Lord, make me truly wise in avoiding harm.

55.   Lord, make my concern that you are not offended.

56.   Lord, make my conversion quick.

57.   Lord, make your power shine
        through my weakness.
58.   Lord, may I hate sinful pleasure.
59.   Lord, may I never be ashamed of the
        true cross.
60.   Lord, may I never seek evil
        compensations.
61.   Lord, may I prefer to suffer than to
        sin.
62.   Lord, my Father, train me, chastise
        me.
63.   Lord, preserve me from sin.
64.   Lord, purify my prayer.
65.   Lord, quench in us the flame of vice
        (Liturgy).
66.   Lord, remove the taint of ill.
67.   Lord, send me the humiliations that
        would make me a saint.
68.   Lord, set thou a seal upon my loins.
69.   Lord, set thou a seal upon my pride.
70.   Lord, sorry. Sorry, Lord, sorry.
71.   Lord, teach me not to forget you.
72.   Lord, wash my head, my hands and
        feet (cf. John 13: 9).
73.   Lord, wound my pride.

74. Mine is to love and suffer (cf. Acts 5: 41).
75. My God, may I hate sin (Blessed Josemaria).
76. O God, be merciful to me a sinner (Luke 18: 13).
77. Purify us, Lord, to give you our best.
78. The Cross Lord, it's my turn.
79. Unload me Lord, that I may fly to you.
80. When I am weak, then I am strong (2Cor. 12: 10).
81. With joy no day without the cross (Blessed Josemaria).

 ## SECTION VI
PETITION 

1. Almighty God, bless us.
2. Guard me as the apple of your eye (Psalm 17: 8).
3. Help me, Lord (cf. Matt. 14: 30).
4. Hide me in the shade of you wings (Psalm 17: 8).
5. Jesus, make me ready.
6. Jesus, Master, have pity on us (Luke 17: 13).
7. Lead us not into temptation (Luke 11: 4).
8. Lord, bless and approve my offering.
9. Lord, bless and approve my work for you.
10. Lord, bless the works of our hands.
11. Lord, bless us in every way.
12. Lord, continue you work in me.
13. Lord, give me a sense of justice.
14. Lord, give me courage for self-knowledge.
15. Lord, give me grace, amazing grace, efficacious grace, operative grace.

16. Lord, give me the wisdom of economics: the economy of time, the economy of means, of ways, and of salvation.
17. Lord, give me time for all.
18. Lord, give us efficacious faith.
19. Lord, give us good humor, clean humor.
20. Lord, give us this bread always (John 6: 34).
21. Lord, graciously bless us.
22. Lord, graciously sanctify all our works.
23. Lord, grant that I may not do anything uselessly.
24. Lord, help me not to waste a second.
25. Lord, help me to act with the authority of humility, of charity, of piety.
26. Lord, help me to finish the work you have given me to do.
27. Lord, help me to pray always.
28. Lord, help me to pray much.
29. Lord, help me to work virtuously.
30. Lord, help us to know the devil's agents.

31. Lord, help us to ride over problems.
32. Lord, I come to draw virtue from you (cf. Luke 8: 46).
33. Lord, I want to run the risk for you.
34. Lord, if you will do so, you can cure me (Matt. 8: 2).
35. Lord, just for today.
36. Lord, keep me safe from those who think badly of me.
37. Lord, keep us safe from Satan and his works and pomp.
38. Lord, lead me unto Glory day by day.
39. Lord, make me a herald of holiness.
40. Lord, make me carry the cross with fear, hope and love.
41. Lord, make me diligent in prayer.
42. Lord, make me economic.
43. Lord, make me fruitful.
44. Lord, make me heroic.
45. Lord, make me hurry up with my work on earth.
46. Lord, make me obey as you want me to.
47. Lord, make me pray better.
48. Lord, make me recognize the devil in

all the ways he comes.

49.   Lord, may all that I do prosper.
50.   Lord, may I never be guilty of malice (cf. 1Thess. 5: 15).
51.   Lord, may I profit from everything.
52.   Lord, may we abound in good works.
53.   Lord, never let me be parted from you (Liturgy).
54.   Lord, save me (Matt. 14: 30).
55.   Lord, show me my wounds.
56.   Lord, show us the Father (John 14: 8).
57.   Lord, speed up your work in me.
58.   Lord, stop me from wasting my life.
59.   Lord, teach me to do my work well.
60.   Lord, teach me when to be still and when to stir.
61.   Lord, teach us to pray (Luke 11: 1).
62.   Lord, thwart the paths of the wicked (cf. Psalms 146: 9; 81: 15; 21: 9).
63.   Lord, what must I do to be saved? (cf. Acts 16: 30)
64.   Lord, work your miracles again.
65.   Lord, your law, your word, your grace, your love: these are my needs each passing moment.

66.   Make us know the brevity of life that
        we may gain wisdom of heart.
67.   My angel, keep me praying.
68.   Save me, O Lord, from the hands of
        the wicked (Psalm 140: 5).
69.   Train me in virtue, Lord.

SECTION VII
HUMILITY

1. Lord, block my way into pride (cf. Jer. 13: 9; 2Cor. 12: 7).
2. Lord, give me the mastery over self that is pleasing to you.
3. Lord, help me to spend each day learning.
4. Lord, make me grow high in humility.
5. Lord, may your blessings never take me away from you.
6. Lord, teach me to look at myself while I try to correct others (cf. Luke 13: 15).
7. Lord, teach me to respect authority and tradition in accordance with your holy will.
8. Make me lowly before you, O Lord.
9. Master, teach me lowliness.
10. Lord, make me so low that you fill me with ease.

1. Father, teach me to live in the reality of the victory of Christ.
2. I'll stick out my neck for you.
3. In Christ there is every ideal.
4. Let your word find home in me.
5. Lord, engrave your Law in me (Romans 2: 15).
6. Lord, fill me with wisdom.
7. Lord, fill us with truth and grace.
8. Lord, give me grace to be thoroughly Christian.
9. Lord, give me light to see your truth in all things.
10. Lord, give me love for the truth.
11. Lord, give me the spirit of the gospels.
12. Lord, give us sound knowledge of the Scriptures, make us accurate in all we teach.
13. Lord, grant me a deep understanding of the malice of sin and the effects of sin.

14. Lord, guided by your gospel, we will live for your Kingdom.
15. Lord, help me believe my defects.
16. Lord, help me to be all that I am meant to be.
17. Lord, help me to consider your law always.
18. Lord, help me to have an eye on the future.
19. Lord, help me to know what is in our nature.
20. Lord, help me to know what's true for me.
21. Lord, help us to recognize our dependency on prayer.
22. Lord, I'd rather be crushed by good than to submit to evil.
23. Lord, in the secret of my heart, teach me wisdom (cf. Job 33: 33; Psalm 51: 8).
24. Lord, keep me in your truth.
25. Lord, keep my head clear for you.
26. Lord, keep us faithful to your teaching (Liturgy).
27. Lord, keep us open to the workings of your Spirit.

28.   Lord, keep us open to your truth
        (2Thess. 2: 10).
29.   Lord, let me defend the truth in all
        things.
30.   Lord, let me distinguish the truth in
        all things.
31.   Lord, let me find you in things that
        are real.
32.   Lord, let me hold the truth in all
        things.
33.   Lord, let me know myself as citizen
        of Heaven.
34.   Lord, let me learn how to live from
        your word.
35.   Lord, let me love the truth in all
        things.
36.   Lord, let me never set myself against
        the truth (cf. John 10: 31).
37.   Lord, let your words abide in me.
38.   Lord, make me aware of my
        limitations.
39.   Lord, make me delicate with your
        law.
40.   Lord, make me do all that I am
        meant to do.

41.   Lord, make me ever more attentive to your gospel.

42.   Lord, make me ever more content.

43.   Lord, make me live in truth and peace.

44.   Lord, make me live the Gospel.

45.   Lord, make me love the truth in all things.

46.   Lord, make me obey all that is holy.

47.   Lord, make me pay constant attention to the brevity of life.

48.   Lord, make me put each thing in its place: wealth, honor, success, fame - in the service of your Kingdom.

49.   Lord, make me quick in accepting truth.

50.   Lord, make me remember the supremacy of prayer.

51.   Lord, make me see the appropriate time.

52.   Lord, make me seek truth.

53.   Lord, make me true to your name, true to your word.

54.   Lord, make me truly Christian.

55.   Lord, make me wise, help me not to live in a dream world.

56.   Lord, make us preserve the truth of your gospel (cf. Gal. 2: 5).
57.   Lord, may I be drawn to the magnet of truth.
58.   Lord, may I never convince myself of anything false or evil.
59.   Lord, may I never ignore my conscience.
60.   Lord, may it be seen in me that I am your child.
61.   Lord, may souls of prayer rule the world.
62.   Lord, reveal yourself to us.
63.   Lord, save us from falsehood (cf. 2Thess. 2: 11).
64.   Lord, show me the season for each thing.
65.   Lord, teach me as on the way to Emmaus (cf. Luke 24: 13-15).
66.   Lord, teach me how to be happier.
67.   Lord, teach me your law.
68.   Make me humble before your truths, O Lord.
69.   Your word is truth, O, Lord!

70.   Your word O Lord, let it be a lamp
        to my feet, a light to my pathway (cf.
        Psalm 119: 105).

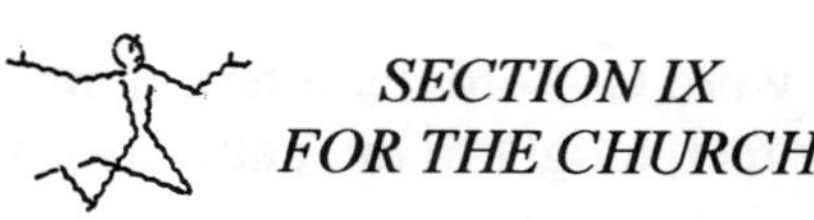

SECTION IX
FOR THE CHURCH

1. Lord, help me to serve you, your Pope and the Holy Mother Church.
2. Lord, help me to serve your Pope, the clergy and all souls.
3. Lord, keep our priests safe.
4. Lord, keep the Bishop safe.
5. Lord, keep the Church a praying Church (cf. Acts 1: 14).
6. Lord, keep the Pope safe.
7. Lord, make me enrich the Church.
8. Lord, thank you for your priests.

SECTION X
APOSTOLIC WITNESS

1. Father, Thy Kingdom come (Luke 11: 2).
2. For me to live is Christ and to die is gain (Phil. 1: 21).
3. Help me to proclaim you by word and deed.
4. I'll make you the best friend of my friends.
5. I'm on a mission from God.
6. Jesus Almighty Healer, help us to use our health or sickness to serve you well.
7. Jesus, make me quick in helping souls.
8. Jesus, multiply the fruits.
9. Jesus, use me.
10. Let me suffer that others may not, Lord.
11. Lord, consecrate them in your truth (John 17: 17).
12. Lord, do not hold the sins against them (cf. Acts 7: 60).

13. Lord, don't let me disturb your work.
14. Lord, engrave your will in me; that all men be saved and come to the knowledge of truth (cf. 1 Tim. 2: 4).
15. Lord, entrust your word to me.
16. Lord, entrust your work to me.
17. Lord, for thy name, thy kingdom and thy will.
18. Lord, give me a missionary sense.
19. Lord, give me a quick interest for each soul.
20. Lord, give me an apostolic mind.
21. Lord, give me apostolic drive, proselytistic drive, evangelical drive.
22. Lord, give me apostolic wisdom, proselytistic wisdom.
23. Lord, give me the joy of seeing your victory in all things.
24. Lord, give us a fighting spirit.
25. Lord, give us deep, operative, militant piety.
26. Lord, give us your temple-cleansing zeal.
27. Lord, grant that I am always being apostolic.

28. Lord, grant that many will be ready for the great and awful day.
29. Lord, help me not to get in your way.
30. Lord, help me to be all things to all men (1Cor. 9: 22).
31. Lord, help me to catch men for you in all the ways they can be caught.
32. Lord, help me to continue your work on earth.
33. Lord, help me to draw good from each person.
34. Lord, help me to know men.
35. Lord, help me to manifest you in all the ways I can to as many souls as possible.
36. Lord, help me to strive that they have life abundantly.
37. Lord, help me to will that all men be saved and attain the knowledge of truth (1Tim. 2: 4).
38. Lord, help us to continue your work on earth.
39. Lord, I love it when you arrange things.
40. Lord, I want to do more.

41. Lord, I want to make you the desire of all the nations.
42. Lord, I want to teach what you teach and as you teach and as you will.
43. Lord, immerse me in the work of salvation.
44. Lord, keep choosing me to accomplish your will.
45. Lord, keep me faithful to your teachings.
46. Lord, keep me going until it is accomplished.
47. Lord, keep the Church on fire as on the day of Pentecost (cf. Acts 2: 3).
48. Lord, keep them true to you name.
49. Lord, lead us to true fidelity, holy fidelity, fruitful fidelity.
50. Lord, let me serve you always with my mind and heart and will.
51. Lord, let me show to others your goodness to me.
52. Lord, let my authority be of humility, of charity, of piety.
53. Lord, make me a herald of holiness in my every word and deed.

54.   Lord, make me a shepherd after your own heart.

55.   Lord, make me all things to all men.

56.   Lord, make me attend to all that matters.

57.   Lord, make me attend to all that's yours.

58.   Lord, make me blaze a trial.

59.   Lord, make me care for the good and salvation of all.

60.   Lord, make me complete in bearing witness to you.

61.   Lord, make me concerned that your banquet hall is filled.

62.   Lord, make me detached from everything while I strive to gain all for you.

63.   Lord, make me do all the apostolate you want me to do.

64.   Lord, make me do all you want of me.

65.   Make me do what is effective to bring people to you.

66.   Lord, make me do what you want me to teach.

67. Lord, make me earnest for the coming of your Kingdom
68. Lord, make me faithful to your call.
69. Lord, make me pass the fruits of my sufferings to others.
70. Lord, make me quick in making friends.
71. Lord, make me sow abundantly the fruits of sanctity.
72. Lord, make me truly missionary.
73. Lord, make us free and happy and fruitful.
74. Lord, make us productive, make us fruitful.
75. Lord, may I never scandalize the goodness in souls.
76. Lord, may nothing dampen my zeal.
77. Lord, may zeal for your house consume me (cf. John 2: 17).
78. Lord, people - make me concerned not about their sin but about their soul.
79. Lord, put your words into my mouth (cf. Jer. 13: 12).
80. Lord, send me.
81. Lord, show us where danger lies.

82. Lord, teach me to look at myself while I try to correct others (Luke 13: 10-17).
83. Lord, teach us how to be fruitful.
84. Lord, teach us to make disciples of all nations (cf. Matt. 28: 19; Acts 1: 8).
85. Lord, teach us what it means to bring others to you.
86. Lord, use me.
87. Lord, we have put aside everything to follow you.
88. Lord, we want to carry out everything you have commanded (Matt. 28: 20).
89. Lord, we will make your house a house of prayer (cf. Mark 11: 17).
90. Lord, woe to me if I do not preach the gospel (cf. 1Cor. 9: 16).
91. Make me earnest for the coming of your Kingdom.
92. Make me strong in bearing witness to you.
93. Protect them from the evil one (John 17: 15; cf. 2Thess. 3: 3).

94. Souls - Lord, make their problems my problems.
95. Speak, Lord! Your servant is listening (cf. 1 Samuel 3: 9).
96. We want Christ to reign.

SECTION XI
ABANDONMENT IN GOD

1. Lord, the Spirit is willing but the flesh is weak (cf. Matt. 26: 41).
2. Father, as you would, not as I would (cf. Matt. 26: 39).
3. Father, I know little, your will be done.
4. Father, into your hands I commend my spirit (Luke 23: 46).
5. Father of mercies! (2Cor. 1: 3).
6. God of peace, be with me.
7. God of all comfort, be with me (cf. 2Cor. 1: 3).
8. Lord, direct me to Heaven.
9. Lord, give me peace and safety.
10. Lord, help me not to oppose you (cf. John 19: 11-28).
11. Lord, help me to will only what you will.
12. Lord, hold me by the hand.
13. Lord, I count on your ruling in all things.
14. Lord, I fear to do my will.

15.   Lord, I want to be so identified with you.
16.   Lord, I will smile through everything.
17.   Lord, if you will.
18.   Lord, justify me.
19.   Lord, make me always dependent on you.
20.   Lord, make me totally dependent on you.
21.   Lord, my food is to do your will (cf. John 4: 34).
22.   Lord of the harvest, help us.
23.   Lord, please arrange things.
24.   Lord, we need your help.
25.   Lord, you know all things.
26.   My God, why have you forsaken me? (Matt. 27: 46; Mark 15: 34).
27.   My God, you astound me!
28.   Omnipotent God, I'm in your hands.
29.   Yes, Lord!
30.   We are strong in the name of the Lord, our God (Psalm 20: 8).

 # SECTION XII
VISION

1. Lord, bless me with vigilance,
    ascetic vigilance, apostolic vigilance.
2. Lord, declare to us the things that are
    to come (cf. John 16: 13).
3. Lord, fill me with wisdom for the
    coming of Your Kingdom.
4. Lord, flood me with your light.
5. Lord, give me a clean conscience.
6. Lord, give me a clear mind.
7. Lord, give me that supernatural
    sensitivity that makes me do the right
    thing at the right time.
8. Lord, give me the vision of wisdom.
9. Lord, give me vision for truth
    always.
10. Lord, give me vision of my mission.
11. Lord, give us light.
12. Lord, give us sound judgement.
13. Lord, help me await you constantly.
14. Lord, help me believe you easily.
15. Lord, help me enrich myself through
    every experience.

16. Lord, help me in each moment to do what I should do.
17. Lord, help me to always perceive what is good, what is true, what is right, what is safe.
18. Lord, help me to know what surpasses knowledge (cf. Eph. 3: 19).
19. Lord, help us to recognize the opportunities you offer (cf. Luke 19: 44).
20. Lord, I need you to show me what I am.
21. Lord, I want to be what you want me to be.
22. Lord, I want to face you each day.
23. Lord, illumine my mind.
24. Lord, lead me to harmony, lead me to glory.
25. Lord, make me faithful to the lights that you give.
26. Lord, make me see what surpasses sight.
27. Lord, make me see!
28. Lord, make me wise in heart and mind and will.
29. Lord, make your gospel clear to me.

30.   Lord, manifest yourself.
31.   Lord, open my heart to know the scriptures (cf. Luke 24: 32).
32.   Lord, reveal to us the mysteries of your Kingdom (cf. Matt. 13: 11; Luke 8: 10).
33.   Lord, reveal what flesh and blood cannot reveal.
34.   Lord, reveal your name, help us to love you (John 17: 26).
35.   Lord, show me what it means to bear fruit (Luke 13: 7).
36.   Lord, show me what victory means.
37.   Lord, show me whatever you want to show me.
38.   Lord, show us where the enemy lies.
39.   Lord, teach me how to be glorious.
40.   Lord, teach me what it means to give you everything that I can.
41.   Lord, teach us to judge wisely the things of the earth (Liturgy).
42.   Now is the time for wisdom.

SECTION XIII
PERFECTION

1. Claim my body, Lord, claim my heart.
2. Jesus, grant us the peace of virtue.
3. Lord, bend my heart to do you will- teach me your law.
4. Lord, fill me with virtue, full measure, pressed down, flowing over (cf. Luke 6: 38).
5. Lord, give me sight to see through falsehood.
6. Lord, give me the power of restraint.
7. Lord, give us efficacious grace.
8. Lord, give us peace in our flesh, in our heart, in our mind.
9. Lord, give us supernatural outlook.
10. Lord, help me always react as a saint would.
11. Lord, help me to be absorbed in prayer.
12. Lord, help me to desire cleanliness.
13. Lord, help me to do everything prayerfully.

14. Lord, help me to finish the work you have given me to do (cf. John 27: 6).
15. Lord, help me to go on prayerfully.
16. Lord, help me to observe all things as a saint should.
17. Lord, help us remove the obstacles to grace.
18. Lord, help us to follow you closely, like the martyrs did.
19. Lord, help us to make progress on the way of salvation (Liturgy).
20. Lord, I plead for merit and virtues.
21. Lord, I want to always walk with you.
22. Lord, I want to be a saint, I want to be a martyr.
23. Lord, I want to run, so make me wise.
24. Lord, keep me balanced in everything.
25. Lord, keep me going virtuously.
26. Lord, keep training me, purify, purge, discipline me.
27. Lord, lead me on to maturity - spiritual and human.

28. Lord, lead me to integrity, lead me to perfection.
29. Lord, lead me to the fullness of joy.
30. Lord, if you let me lose anything, don't let me lose you.
31. Lord, let me reflect with my life, all that belongs to you my Father God.
32. Lord, let the activity of my being be holy, pleasing to you, and meritorious.
33. Lord, let your Spirit rest heavily upon us.
34. Lord, like you did, let me do.
35. Lord, make a saint out of this wretch (Blessed Josemaria).
36. Lord, make me a temple of your Holy Spirit.
37. Lord, make me attentive to your Spirit.
38. Lord, make me completely dependent on you.
39. Lord, make me good, make me really good.
40. Lord, make me live the Gospel to the full.
41. Lord, make me live the Holy Mass.

42.   Lord, make me love virtue.
43.   Lord, make me meticulous in
        avoiding sin.
44.   Lord, make me perceive as saints
        perceive.
45.   Lord, make me pray the best way.
46.   Lord, make me recall your life in
        each event of my life
47.   Lord, make me stand firm to the end.
48.   Lord, make me steadfast in prayer,
        steadfast in mortification, steadfast
        on apostolate, steadfast in service.
49.   Lord, make me view everything in
        the perspective of holiness.
50.   Lord, make me walk in the Spirit.
51.   Lord, make my life a harmony.
52.   Lord, make us pay heed to the
        Gospel – all the Gospel.
53.   Lord, may I always insist on being
        better each day.
54.   Lord, may I enjoy your favor.
55.   Lord, may my footsteps be firm in
        keeping your commandments.
56.   Lord, may our works lead us to
        perfection and may our piety
        produce good works.

57. Lord, show us where danger lies.
58. Lord, take me at the holiest moment of my life.
59. My God, keep my soul fit!
60. My prestige is your glory, Lord.

SECTION XIV
OUR LADY

1. Mary, be always my loving Mother.
2. Mother! Help me to let it be!
3. Mother, ask God for me, for those graces I do not know of.
4. Mother, grant that I'm bringing many souls to Heaven.
5. Mother, help me not to miss a single prompting of the Holy Spirit.
6. Mother, help me respond to God's favors with humility and gratitude.
7. Mother, help me to be a child of God as you are.
8. Mother, help me to be about my Father's business (cf. Luke 2: 49).
9. Mother, help me to be totally available to love.
10. Mother, help me to be totally responsive to love.
11. Mother, help me to enjoy God's favor.
12. Mother, help me to know what offends Him.

13. Mother, help me to love God as you love him.
14. Mother, help me to receive God's graces.
15. Mother, I want to be His!
16. Mother, I want to steer clear of sin.
17. Mother, keep me close to God.

COMMUNION OF SAINTS

The Communion of Saints is a great treasure of the Catholic Church and of all true Christians, members of the Mystical Body of Christ which transcends all races, all times, and all places. The Family of God cannot be viewed in terms of time and space but with the light of faith and love, and thus we know we are in communion with all our brethren in this world and in the next. We therefore cannot and do not separate the militant Church on earth, the suffering Souls in Purgatory and the triumphant Saints in Heaven (1Cor. 12: 12; Heb. 12: 22-24). This catholic fellowship is not a creation of man, but a natural consequence of Family Life of the Church. We are in communion with one another on earth by sharing the same faith and doctrine. These we receive from the Hierarchy of the Church, the "Pillar and Bulwark of Truth" (1Tim. 3: 15), established by Christ and not by men (Matt. 16: 18-19; 28: 19-20; John 21: 15-17; Luke 22: 32). The Church exists to keep men from religious error till the end of time (Matt. 16: 19; John 14: 16-26; Matt. 28: 20; Luke 10: 16) and to supply the militant Church with all its needs, chiefly the sacraments (John 20: 23; Luke 22: 19; John 6: 58-59; James 5: 14, 15). We honor our triumphant brethren at home with the Lord Jesus Christ (1Cor. 12: 26; 2Cor. 5: 8; Phil. 1: 23) (more than we honor any human being on earth for any achievement); we borrow from their experience, and ask them for their help (1Cor. 12: 21, 25), because we know they are concerned about us (Luke 15: 10; Rev. 5: 8): they have power over the earth (Rev. 2: 26; 5: 10). As we believe in the mercy and justice of Omnipotent God, (Matt. 16: 27; Matt. 19: 25-26), we are bound to help our suffering brethren in Purgatory (1Cor. 12: 26; 2Macc. 12: 46) to be through with their purification ("salvation by fire", 1Cor. 3: 15; "forgiveness in the world to come", Matt. 12: 32), and join the Saints in Heaven since we know nothing defiled shall enter Heaven (Rev. 21: 27).

Each of us will make our own special friends among the Angels and Saints and keep our own private devotions; but it is a better sign of the communion of Saints that we follow the Liturgical Calendar. We find it in our Missals, and it is presented to us in daily Mass.

Below are some popular prayers of Christian tradition and a list of the more important saints remembered for their great contributions to the growth of the Church: the Doctors of the Church (for their doctrine) and the Martyrs (who died for the faith). Of course there are many more popular saints many of whom were founders of communities within the Church such as St Ignatius of Loyola, St Dominic, St Francis of Assisi or those that are Patrons for specific purposes such as St John Vianney - Patron of the Universal Clergy. These are all presented to us in the Missal and we can develop our own devotion to them remembering that creatures - including saints - cannot displace God, but are for us a reflection of the goodness of God, the unity of God's Family and an evidence of the power of God's grace in his creatures.

The companionships of the angels is a great treasure: "For to his angels he has given command about you that they guard you in all your ways" (Psalm 91: 11; Gen. 24: 7; Ex. 23: 20; Psalm 34: 8).

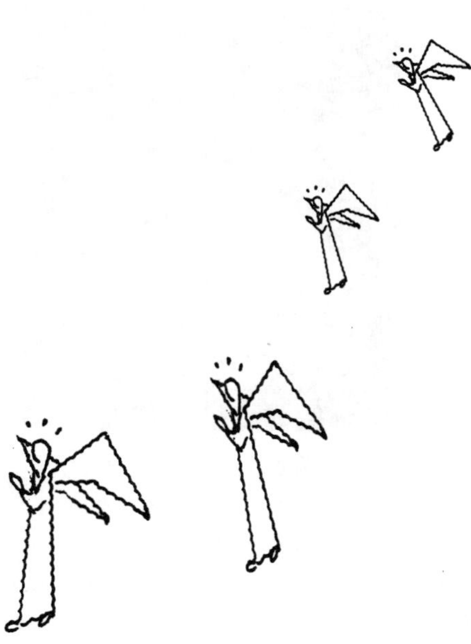

DEVOTION TO THE BLESSED VIRGIN MARY

" ... Henceforth all generations shall call me blessed" (Luke 1: 48)

The five joyful mysteries

The Annunciation.

Mary receives the Angel's message. We too must learn to keep silent often, to pray, to keep in the presence of God, to discover the Will of God which is often hidden by the hustle and bustle of life. *Mother, pray for us that everyday, in every way, through everything, we may get to know God.*

The Visitation.

Mary visits Elizabeth. Like Mary, we must learn to give ourselves to others; to serve; to take Christ to them. *Mother, pray for us that the human family will be strengthened and sanctified by the Christian spirit we bear.*

The Nativity.

Mary gives birth to Jesus. Like Mary, we too have our role to play in giving Christ to the world. *Mother, we want to do as you did.*

The Presentation.

Mary and Joseph go to fulfil the Mosaic Law. When we fulfil God's law, he uses us to take the Savior to many who wait in expectation and we fill the world with hope and joy. *Mother, pray for us that we may be eager to fulfil God's law.*

The Finding in the Temple.

Mary and Joseph find Jesus in the temple. Jesus teaches us the most important thing: God's business; teaching the truth; the work of salvation; eternal life. Our Lady will help us to do whatever God tells us. *Mother, pray for us so that we do not waste our time on worthless matters.*

The five sorrowful mysteries

The Agony in the Garden.

Jesus prays before His crucifixion.   Like Jesus, we too must pray through everything. That is how to face our lives. *Mother, help us to abide in Him through all our trials and temptations.*

The Scourging at the Pillar.
Jesus is scourged by the soldiers. Remembering Jesus, we will learn to bear the scourges of each day fruitfully. *Mother, help us not to waste God's graces.*

The Crowning with Thorns.
Jesus is crowned in mockery. *Ecce Homo!* Behold the man! Son of God! But how we like to show how great we are. We must learn from Him about humility. *Mother, help us to show how good God is.*

The Carrying of the Cross.

Jesus carries the cross to Calvary. He has said we must take up our cross daily to follow him. We pray for grace to carry the cross with the dignity of faith, of hope, and of love. *Mother, help us on our way.*

The Crucifixion.

Jesus is crucified between sinners. The Redemption is ours but we know that to claim that victory, we must die to self and to sin. Thus we live a new life in Him. *Mother, help us in our battle to overcome sin.*

The five glorious mysteries

The Resurrection.

Jesus is risen! There is our hope. We too can now rise from sin in this world and from death in the next. *Mother, help us to live in the reality of the victory of Christ.*

The Ascension.
Jesus ascends to Heaven. He lives to reign!
We will gladly follow him to eternal life.
Mother, help us to enjoy a foretaste of that glory.

The Descent of the Holy Spirit.

What a consolation to know that the Holy Spirit is with the Church on earth till the end of time. *Mother, pray for us that we may live our new life to the full.*

The Assumption.

Mary is taken up into Heaven. She will help us not to miss the way to Heaven. *Mother, help us to keep our gaze heavenward.*

The Coronation of Our Lady.

Mary is Queen of Heaven. She is also our mother. She will help us to do our work on earth well and to bring other souls to Heaven! *Mother, obtain for us the mercies of God*

Litany of the Blessed Virgin

Lord, have mercy on us.
Lord, have mercy on us.
Christ, have mercy on us.
Christ, have mercy on us.
Lord, have mercy on us.
Lord, have mercy on us.
Christ, hear us.
Christ, graciously hear us.
God the Father of heaven
Have mercy on us.
God the Son, redeemer of the world
Have mercy on us.
God the Holy Spirit
Have mercy on us.
Holy Trinity, one God
Have mercy on us.

Holy Mary	Pray for us
Holy Mother of God	"
Holy Virgin of virgins	"
Mother of Christ	"
Mother of the Church	"
Mother of Divine Grace	"
Mother most pure	"
Mother most chaste	"
Mother inviolate	"
Mother undefiled	"
Mother immaculate	"
Mother most amiable	"
Mother most admirable	"
Mother of good counsel	"
Mother of our Creator	"
Mother of our Savior	"
Virgin most prudent	"
Virgin most venerable	"
Virgin most renowned	"

Virgin most powerful	"
Virgin most merciful	"
Virgin most faithful	"
Mirror of justice	"
Seat of wisdom	"
Cause of our joy	"
Spiritual vessel	"
Vessel of honor	"
Singular vessel of devotion	"
Mystical rose	"
Tower of David	"
Tower of ivory	"
House of gold	"
Ark of the Covenant	"
Gate of Heaven	"
Morning star	"
Health of the sick	"
Refuge of sinners	"
Comforter of the afflicted	"
Help of Christians	"
Queen of angels	"
Queen of patriarchs	"
Queen of prophets	"
Queen of apostles	"
Queen of martyrs	"
Queen of confessors	"
Queen of virgins	"
Queen of all saints	"
Queen conceived without original sin	"
Queen assumed into Heaven	"
Queen of the most holy rosary	"
Queen of the family	"
Queen of peace	"

Lamb of God, who takes away the sins of the world; *spare us, O Lord.*
Lamb of God who takes away the sins of the world; *graciously hear us, O Lord.*
Lamb of God who takes away the sins of the world; *have mercy on us.*

Pray for us, O holy Mother of God; *that we may be made worthy of the promises of Christ.*

Prayer:
O God, whose only begotten Son, by His life, death and resurrection, has purchased for us the rewards of Eternal Life; grant, we beseech you, that while meditating on these mysteries of the most holy Rosary of the Blessed Virgin Mary, we may imitate what they contain and obtain what they promise, through the same Christ Our Lord. Amen.

For the Church and State:
Our Father, Hail Mary and Glory be
For the Bishop:
Our Father, Hail Mary and Glory be
For Holy Souls in purgatory:
Our Father, Hail Mary
May they rest in peace, *Amen.*

Hail Holy Queen

Hail Holy Queen, Mother of mercy;
Hail, our life, our sweetness, and our hope!
To you do we cry,
Poor banished children of Eve;
To you do we send up our sighs,
Mourning and weeping
In this vale of tears.
Turn then, most gracious advocate,
Your eyes of mercy towards us;
And after this our exile,
Show to us the blessed fruit of your womb,
Jesus.
O clement, O loving, O sweet Virgin Mary.
Pray for us O holy Mother of God.
That we may be made worthy of the
Promises of Christ.
Amen.

The Angelus

The Angel of the Lord declared to Mary:
And she conceived of the Holy Spirit.
Hail Mary...

Behold the handmaid of the Lord:
Be it done to me according to your word.
Hail Mary…

And the Word was made flesh:
And dwelt among us.
Hail Mary...

Pray for us, O Holy Mother of God:
That we may be made worthy of the
promises of Christ.

Prayer:
Pour forth, we beseech you, O Lord, your grace into our hearts, that we to whom the Incarnation of Christ, your Son, was made known by the message of an angel, may be brought by his passion and cross to the glory of his resurrection, through the same Christ our Lord. Amen.

The Regina Caeli

Queen of Heaven, rejoice! *Alleluia!*
For He whom you did merit to bear,
Alleluia!
Has risen as He said. *Alleluia!*
Pray for us to God. *Alleluia!*
Rejoice and be glad O Virgin Mary,
Alleluia!
For the Lord has risen indeed. *Alleluia!*

Prayer:

O God who gave joy to the whole world through the resurrection of your Son our Lord Jesus Christ, grant that we may obtain, through his Virgin Mother, Mary, the joys of everlasting life: through the same Christ our Lord. Amen.

The Memorarae

Remember, O most loving Virgin Mary,
That it is a thing unheard of,
That anyone ever had recourse
To your protection,
Implored your help,
Or sought your intercession,
And was left forsaken.
Filled therefore with confidence
In your goodness
I fly to you, O Mother,
Virgin of Virgins.
To you I come,
Before you I stand,
A sorrowful sinner.
Despise not my poor words,
O Mother of the Word of God,
But graciously hear and grant my prayer.
Amen.

The Magnificat

My soul magnifies the Lord,
And my spirit rejoices
In God my Savior,
For he has regarded
The low estate of his handmaiden.
For behold henceforth
All generations will call me blessed;
For He who is mighty
Has done great things for me,
And Holy is His Name.
And his mercy is on those who fear him
From generation to generation.
He has shown strength with his arm,
He has scattered the proud
In the imagination of their hearts;
He has put down the mighty
From their thrones,
And exalted those of low degree.
He has filled the hungry with good things,
And the rich he has sent empty away.
He has helped his servant, Israel,
In remembrance of his mercy,
As he spoke to our fathers,
To Abraham and to his posterity forever.

Prayer to Our Lady

Hail Mary! Full of grace!
What a privilege you bear;
Purest of women,
Virgin Mother,
Most highly favored of our race!
By your triple advantage:
Daughter of God the Father,
Mother of God the Son
Spouse of the Holy Spirit,
Obtain from God on our behalf
Those graces we know little or naught about.
And so, Dear Mother,
Blest through thee,
Our lives will manifest His Will. Amen.

Commendation

Jesus, Mary and Joseph, I give you my heart
and my soul.
Jesus, Mary and Joseph, assist me in my last
agony.
Jesus, Mary and Joseph, may I breathe forth
my soul in peace with you. Amen.

LITANY OF THE SAINTS
This may be said to accompany a dying person.

Lord, have mercy	Lord, have mercy
Christ, have mercy	Christ, have mercy
Lord, have mercy	Lord, have mercy
Holy Mary, Mother of God	Pray for us
Holy Angels of God	"
Abraham, our Father in Faith	"
David, leader of God's people	"
All holy patriarchs and prophets	"
Saint John the Baptist	"
Saint Joseph	"
Saint Peter and Saint Paul	"
Saint Andrew	"
Saint John	"
Saint Mary Magdalene	"
Saint Stephen	"
Saint Ignatius	"
Saint Lawrence	"
Saint Perpetua and Saint Felicity	"
Saint Agnes	"
Saint Gregory	"
Saint Augustine	"
Saint Athanasius	"
Saint Basil	"
Saint Martin	"
Saint Benedict	"
Saint Francis and Saint Dominic	"
Saint Francis Xavier	"
Saint John Vianney	"
Saint Catherine	"
Saint Theresa	"
All holy men and women	"
Lord, be merciful	Lord, save your people
From all evil	"
From every sin	"
From Satan's power	"

At the moment of death	"
From everlasting death	"
On the day of judgement	"
By your coming as man	"
By your suffering and cross	"
By your death and rising to new life	"
By your return in Glory to the Father	"
By your gift of the Holy Spirit	"
By your coming again in Glory	"
Be merciful to us sinners	Lord, hear our prayer
Bring us to the eternal Life first promised to us in Baptism	"
Raise us on the last day, for we have eaten the Bread of Life	"
Let us share in your glory, for we have shared in your suffering and death	"
Jesus, son of the Living God	"
Christ hear us	Christ hear us
Lord Jesus, hear our prayer	Lord Jesus, hear our prayer

FOR THE FAITHFUL DEPARTED

Psalm 130
Out of the depths I have cried to you,
O Lord;
Lord, hear my voice.
Let your ears be attentive
To the voice of my supplication.
If you, O Lord,
Shall observe iniquities,
Lord, who shall endure it?
For with you there is merciful forgiveness:
And by reason of your law
I have waited for you, O Lord.
My soul has relied on his word;
My soul has hoped in the Lord.
From the morning watch
Even until night,
Let Israel hope in the Lord.
Because with the Lord there is mercy,
And with him plentiful redemption.
And he shall redeem Israel
From all his iniquities.
Eternal rest grant to them, O Lord.
And let perpetual light shine on them.
May they rest in peace.

Amen.
Lord, hear my prayer.
And let my cry come to you.

Prayer:

O God, the Creator and Redeemer of all the Faithful, grant to the souls of your servants departed the remission of all their sins, that through our pious supplication they may obtain that pardon which they have always desired; who lives and reigns for ever and ever. Amen.

PRAYER TO RELEASE SOULS FROM PURGATORY

Eternal Father, I offer Thee
The most Precious Blood of
Thy Divine Son, Jesus
In union with the Masses
Said throughout the world today
For all the Holy Souls in Purgatory;
For sinners everywhere;
For sinners in the universal Church -
Those in my own home
And within my family

(Indulgence to release 1000 souls from Purgatory on November 16, Feast of St Gertrude)

THE THREE ARCHANGELS
(Feast day: 29th September)
St Michael
St Gabriel
St Raphael

PRAYER TO ST MICHAEL
Saint Michael the Archangel,
Defend us in battle.
Be our protection
Against the wickedness
And snares of the devil.
May God rebuke him, we humbly pray;
And do thou O Prince of the Heavenly Host,
By the power of God, thrust into hell
Satan and all evil spirits
Who wander through the world
For the ruin of souls. Amen.

SOME OF THE SAINTS IN HEAVEN AND THEIR LITURGICAL FEASTS

St Joseph, husband of Mary, 19th March. Also celebrated as St Joseph the Worker, 1st May

THE TWELVE APOSTLES
St Peter, the first Head of the Church on earth (Pope), 29th June
St Andrew, brother of St Peter, 30th Nov
St James, the Greater, son of Zebedee, 25th July
St John, son of Zebedee, 27th Dec
St Philip, 3rd May
St Bartholomew, 24th Aug
St Matthew, tax collector, 21st Sept
St Thomas, doubting Thomas, 3rd July
St James the Less, son of Alphaeus cousin of our Lord, 3rd May
St Simon, the Zealot, 28th Oct
St Jude Thaddeus, 28th Oct
St Matthias, who replaced the apostle Judas, 14th May

THE FOUR EVANGELISTS
St Matthew, 21st Sept
St Mark, 25th April
St Luke, 18th Oct
St John, 27th Dec

OTHER APOSTLES
St Paul, Apostle of the Gentiles, 29th June
St Barnabas, 11th June
St Timothy, 26th Jan
St Titus, 26th Jan

FRIENDS OF JESUS
St Mary Magdalene, 22nd July
St Martha, 29th July

DOCTORS OF THE CHURCH
St Basil the Great, 2nd Jan
St Gregory Nazianzen, 2nd Jan
St Hilary, 13th Jan
St Francis de Sales, 24th Jan
St Thomas Aquinas, 28th Jan
St Damian, 21st Feb
St Cyril of Jerusalem, 18th March
St Isidore, 4th April
St Anselm, 21st April

St Catherine of Sienna, 29th April
St Athanasius, 2nd May
St Bede, 25 May
St Ephrem, 9th June
St Anthony of Padua, Evangelical Doctor,
13th June
St Cyril of Alexandria, 27 June
St Bonaventure, 15th July
St Lawrence of Brindisi, 21 July
St Chrysologus, 30th July
St Alphonsus Liguori, 1st Aug
St Lawrence, 10th Aug
St Bernard, 20th Aug
St Augustine of Hippo, 28th Aug
St Gregory the Great, 3rd Sept
St John Chrysostom, 13th Sept
St Robert Bellarmine, 17th Sept
St Jerome, 30th Sept
St Teresa of the Child Jesus, 1st Oct
St Theresa of Avila, 15th Oct
St Leo the Great, 10th Nov
St John Damascene, 4th Dec
St Ambrose, 7th Dec
St John of the Cross, 14th Dec
St Peter Canisius, 21st Dec

THE MARTYRS
St Fabian, 20th Jan
St Sebastian, 20th Jan
St Agnes, 21st Jan
St Vincent, 22nd Jan
St Blaise, 3rd Feb
St Agatha, 5th Feb
St Paul Miki & Co, 6th Feb
St Polycarp, 23rd Feb
St Pepetua,7th March
St Felicity, 7th March
St Stanislaus, 11th April
St Martin I, 13th April
St George, 23rd April
St Fidelis, 24th April
St Peter Chanel, 28th April
St Nereus, 12th May
St Achilleus, 12th May
St Pancras, 12th May
St John I, 18th May
St Justin, 1st June
St Marcellinus, 2nd June
St Peter, 2nd June
St Charles Lwanga & Co, 3rd June
St Boniface, 5th June
St John Fisher, 22nd June

St Thomas More, 22nd June
St Irenaeus, 28th June
St Maria Goretti, 6th July
St Sixtus II, 7th Aug
St Pontian, 13th Aug
St Hippolytus, 13th Aug
St Maximilian Mary Kolbe, 14th Aug
St Cornelius, 16th Sept
St Cyprian, 16th Sept
St Januarius, 19th Sept
St Andrew Kim Taegon, 20th Sept
St Paul Chong Hosang, 20th Sept
St Cosmas, 26th Sept
St Damian, 26th Sept
St Wenceslaus, 28th Sept
St Lorenzo Ruiz & Co, 28th Sept
St Denis & Co, 9th Oct
St Callistus I, 14th Oct
St John de Brebeuf, 19th Oct
St Isaac Jogues, 19th Oct
St Josaphat, 12th Nov
St Cecilia, 22nd Nov
St Clement I, 23rd Nov
St Lucy, 13th Dec
St Stephen, 26th Dec
St Thomas Becket, 29th Dec

SELECTED PSALMS

DESIRE FOR GOD

PSALM 42

As the dear longs for running waters,
So my soul longs for you, O God.
Athirst is my soul for God, the living God.
When shall I go and behold the face of God?
My tears are my food day and night,
As they say to me day after day,
"Where is your God?"
Those times I recall,
Now that I pour out my soul within me,
When I went with the throng
And led them in procession
To the house of God,
Amid loud cries of joy and thanksgiving,
With the multitude keeping festival.
Why are you so downcast O my soul?
Why do you sigh within me?
Hope in God!
For I shall again be thanking him,
In the presence of my savior and my God.

PSALM 63

O God, you are my God whom I seek;
For you my flesh pines
And my soul thirsts.
Like the earth, parched,
Lifeless and without water.
Thus have I gazed toward you
In the sanctuary
To see your power and your glory,
For your kindness is a greater good than life;
My lips shall glorify you.
Thus will I bless you while I live;
Lifting up my hands,
I will call upon your name.
As with the riches of a banquet shall
My soul be satisfied,
And with exultant lips
My mouth shall praise you.
I will remember you upon my couch,
And through the night-watches
I will meditate on you:
That you are my help,
And in the shadow of your wings
I shout for joy.
My soul clings fast to you;
Your right hand upholds me.

WORSHIP AND PRAISE

PSALM 8

O Lord, our Lord,
How glorious is your name
Over all the earth!
You have exalted your majesty
Above the heavens.
Out of the mouths of babes and sucklings
You have fashioned praise
Because of your foes,
To silence the hostile and the vengeful.
When I behold your heavens,
The work of your fingers,
The moon and the stars
Which you set in place –
What is man that you
Should be mindful of him,
Or the son of man that you
Should care for him?
You have made him
Little less than the angels,
And crowned him with glory and honor.
You have given him rule over
The works of your hands,
Putting all things under his feet:

All sheep and oxen,
Yes, and the beasts of the field,
The birds of the air, the fishes of the sea,
And whatever swims the paths of the seas.
O Lord, our Lord,
How glorious is your name
Over all the earth!

PSALM 145

I will extol you,
O God my King,
And I will bless your name forever and ever.
Every day will I bless you,
And I will praise your name
Forever and ever.
Great is the Lord and highly to be praised;
His greatness is unsearchable.
Generation after generation
Praises your works
And proclaims your might.
They speak of the
Splendor of your glorious majesty
And tell of your wondrous works.
They discourse of the power
Of your terrible deeds
And declare your greatness.

They publish the fame of
Your abundant goodness
And joyfully sing of your justice.
The Lord is gracious and merciful,
Slow to anger and of great kindness.
The Lord is good to all
And compassionate toward all his works.
Let all your works give you thanks, O Lord,
And let your faithful ones bless you.

PSALM 148

Praise the Lord from the heavens,
Praise him in the heights;
Praise him, all you his angels
Praise him all you his hosts.
Praise him, sun and moon;
Praise him, all you shining stars.
Praise him, you highest heavens,
And you, waters above the heavens.
Let them praise the name of the Lord,
For he commanded and they were created;
He established them forever and ever;
He gave them a duty,
Which shall not pass away.
Praise the Lord from the earth,
You sea monsters and all depths;

Fire and hail, snow and mist,
Storm winds that fulfil his word;
You mountains and all you hills,
You fruit trees and all you cedars;
You wild beasts and all tame animals,
You creeping things and all you fowl.
Let the kings of the earth
And all you peoples,
The princes and all the judges of the earth,
Young men too and maidens,
Old men and boys,
Praise the name of the Lord,
For his name alone is exalted;
His majesty is above earth and heaven,
And he has lifted up the horn of his people.
Be this his praise from all his faithful ones,
From the children of Israel,
The people close to him. Alleluia.

THANKS

PSALM 18

I love you, O Lord, my strength,
O Lord, my rock, my fortress, my deliverer.
My God, my rock of refuge,
My shield, the horn of my salvation,

My stronghold!
Praised be the Lord, I exclaimed,
And I am safe from my enemies.
For who is God except the Lord?
Who is a rock, save our God?
The God who girded me with strength
And kept my way unerring;
Who made my feet swift as those of hinds
And set me on the heights;
Who trained my hands for war
And my arms to bend a bow of brass.
You have given me your saving shield;
Your right hand has upheld me,
And you have stooped to make me great.
The Lord live!
And blessed be my Rock!
Extolled be God my savior.

PSALM 34

I will bless the Lord at all times;
His praise shall be ever in my mouth.
Let my soul glory in the Lord;
The lowly will hear me and be glad.
Glorify the Lord with me,
Let us together extol his name.
I sought the Lord, and he answered me

And delivered me from all my fears.
Look to him
That you may be radiant with joy,
And your faces may not blush with shame.
When the afflicted man called,
The Lord heard,
And from all his distress he saved him.
The angel of the Lord encamps
Around those who fear him,
And delivers them.
Taste and see how good the Lord is;
Happy the man who takes refuge in him.

PSALM 92

It is good to give thanks to the Lord,
To sing praise to your name, Most High,
To proclaim your kindness at dawn
And your faithfulness throughout the night,
With ten-stringed instrument and lyre,
With melody upon the harp.
For you make me glad,
O Lord, by your deeds;
At the works of your hands I rejoice.
How great are your works, O Lord!
How very deep are your thoughts!
A senseless man knows not,

Nor does a fool understand this.
Though the wicked flourish like grass
And all evil doers thrive,
They are destined for eternal destruction;
While you O Lord,
Are the Most High forever.

PSALM 136

Give thanks to the Lord for he is good,
For his mercy endures forever;
Give thanks to the God of gods,
For his mercy endures forever;
Give thanks to the Lord of lords,
For his mercy endures forever;
Who alone does great wonders,
For his mercy endures forever;
Who made the heavens in wisdom,
For his mercy endures forever;
Who spread out the earth upon the waters,
For his mercy endures forever;
Who made the great lights,
For is mercy endures forever;
The sun to rule over the day,
For his mercy endures forever;
The moon and stars to rule over the night,
For his mercy endures forever;

Who remembered us in our abjection,
For his mercy endures forever;
And freed us from our foes,
For his mercy endures forever;
Who gives food to all flesh,
For his mercy endures forever.
Give thanks to the God of heaven,
For his mercy endures forever.

HIS LAW

PSALM 19

The law of the Lord is perfect,
Refreshing the soul;
The decree of the Lord is trustworthy,
Giving wisdom to the simple.
The precepts of the Lord are right,
Rejoicing the heart;
The command of the Lord is clear,
Enlightening the eye;
The fear of the Lord is pure,
Enduring forever,
The ordinances of the Lord are true,
All of them just;
They are more precious than gold;
Than a heap of purest gold;

Sweeter also than syrup
Or honey from the comb.
Though your servant is careful of them,
Very diligent in keeping them,
Yet who can detect failings?
Cleanse me from my unknown faults!
From wanton sin especially
Restrain your servant;
Let it not rule over me.
Then shall I be blameless
And innocent of serious sin.
Let the words of my mouth
And the thought of my heart
Find favor before you,
O Lord, my rock and my redeemer.

PSALM 119

Happy are they whose way is blameless
Who walk in the law of the Lord.
Happy are they who observe his decrees,
Who seek him with all their heart,
And do no wrong,
But walk in his ways.
You have commanded that your precepts
Be diligently kept.
Oh, that I might be firm in the ways

Of keeping your statutes!
Then should I not be put to shame
When I beheld all your commands.
I will give you thanks with an upright heart,
When I have learnt your just ordinances.
I will keep your statutes;
Do not utterly forsake me.
Instruct me, O Lord,
In the way of your statutes,
That I may exactly observe them.
Give me discernment,
That I may observe your law
And keep it with all my heart.
Lead me in the path of your commands,
For in it I delight.
Incline my heart to your decrees
And not to gain.
Turn away my eyes
From seeing what is vain;
By your way give me life.
Fulfil for your servant
Your promises to those who fear you.
Turn away from me the reproach,
Which I dread
For your ordinances are good.
Behold, I long for your precepts;

In your justice give me life.
Had not your law been my delight,
I should have perished in my affliction
A lamp to my feet is your word,
A light to my path.
Those who love your law have great peace,
And for them there is no stumbling block.
I wait for your salvation, O Lord,
And your commands I fulfil.
I keep your decrees and love them deeply.
I keep your precepts and your decrees,
For all my ways are before you.

BLESSING

PSALM 67

May God have pity on us and bless us.
May He let his face shine upon us.
So may your way be known upon earth;
Among all nations, your salvation.
May the peoples praise you, O God;
May all the peoples praise you!
May the nations be glad and exult
Because you rule the peoples with equity;
The nations on the earth you guide.
May the peoples praise you, O God;

May all the peoples praise you!
The earth has yielded its fruits;
God, our God has blessed us,
And may all the ends of the earth fear him!

TRUST AND CONFIDENCE

PSALM 16

Keep me, O God, for in you I take refuge;
I say to the Lord, "My Lord are you.
Apart from you I have no good"
How wonderfully has he made me cherish
The holy ones who are in his land!
They multiply their sorrows
Who court other gods.
Blood libations to them I will not pour out,
Nor will I take their names upon my lips.
O Lord, my allotted portion and my cup,
You it is who hold fast my lot.
For me the measuring lines have fallen
On pleasant sites;
Fair to me indeed is my inheritance.
I bless the Lord who counsels me;
Even in the night my heart exhorts me.
I set the Lord ever before me;
With him at my right hand

I shall not be disturbed.
Therefore my heart is glad
And my soul rejoices,
My body too abides in confidence;
Because you will not abandon my soul
To the nether world,
Nor will you suffer your faithful one
To undergo corruption.
You will show me the path to life,
Fullness of joys in your presence,
The delights at your right hand forever.

PSALM 27

The Lord is my light and my salvation;
Whom should I fear?
The Lord is my life's refuge;
Of whom should I be afraid?
When evildoers come at me
To devour my flesh,
My foes and my enemies
Themselves stumble and fall.
Though an army encamps against me,
My heart will not fear;
Though war be waged upon me,
Even then will I trust.
One thing I ask of the Lord;

This I seek:
To dwell in the house of the Lord
All the days of my life,
That I may gaze on
The loveliness of the Lord
And contemplate his temple
For he will hide me in his abode
In the day of trouble;
He will conceal me in the shelter of his tent,
He will set me high upon a rock.
Even now my head is held high
Above my enemies on every side.
And I will offer in his tent
Sacrifices with shouts of gladness;
I will sing and chant praise to the Lord.

PSALM 131

O Lord, my heart is not proud,
Nor are my eyes haughty;
I busy not myself with great things,
Nor with things too sublime for me.
Nay rather, I have stilled and quieted
My soul like a weaned child.
Like a weaned child on its mother's lap,
So is my soul within me.
O Israel, hope in the Lord,

Both now and forever.

GUIDANCE AND HELP

PSALM 23
The Lord is my shepherd;
I shall not want.
In verdant pastures he gives me repose;
Besides restful waters he leads me;
He refreshes my soul.
He guides me in right paths
For his name sake.
Even though I walk in the dark valley
I fear no evil;
For you are at my side
With your rod and your staff
That give me courage.
You spread the table before me
In the sight of my foes;
You anoint my head with oil;
My cup overflows.
Only goodness and kindness follow me
All the days of my life;
And I shall dwell in the house of the Lord
For years to come.

PSALM 25

To you I lift up my soul,
O Lord, my God,
In you I trust; let me not be put to shame,
Let not my enemies exult over me.
No one who waits for you
Shall be put to shame;
Those shall be put to shame
Who heedlessly break faith.
Your ways, O Lord, make known to me;
Teach me your paths,
Guide me in your truth and teach me,
For you are God my savior,
And for you I wait all day.
Remember that your compassion, O Lord,
And your kindness are from of old.
The sins of my youth and my frailties
Remember not;
In your kindness remember me
Because of your goodness. O Lord.

PSALM 71

In you, O Lord, I take refuge;
Let me never be put to shame.
In your justice rescue me, and deliver me;
Incline your ear to me, and save me.
Be my rock of refuge,
A stronghold to give me safety,
For you are my rock and my fortress.
O my God, rescue me from the hand of the
wicked,
From the grasp of the criminal and violent.
For you are my hope, O Lord;
My trust, O God, from my youth.
On you I depend from birth;
From my mother's womb you are my
strength;
Constant has been my hope in you.
A portent am I to many,
But you are my strong refuge!
My mouth shall be filled with your praise,
With your glory day by day.
Cast me not off in my old age;
As my strength fails, forsake me not,
My mouth shall declare your justice
Day by day your salvation,
Though I know not their extent

I will treat of the mighty works of the Lord;
O God, I will tell of your singular justice.

PSALM 121

I lift up my eyes towards the mountain;
Whence shall help come to me?
My help is from the Lord,
Who made heaven and earth.
May he not suffer your foot to slip;
May he slumber not who guides you:
Indeed he neither slumbers nor sleeps;
The guardian of Israel.
The Lord is your guardian;
The Lord is your shade;
He is beside you at your right hand.
The sun shall not harm you by day,
Nor the moon by night.
The Lord will guard you from all evil
He will guard your life.
The Lord will guard your coming
And your going,
Both now and forever.

ABANDONMENT IN GOD

PSALM 62

Only in God be at rest, my soul,
For from him comes my hope
He only is my rock and my salvation,
My stronghold; I shall not be disturbed.
With God is my safety and my glory,
He is the rock of my strength;
My refuge is in my God.
Trust in him at all times,
O my people!
Pour out your hearts before him;
God is our refuge!

PSALM 139

O Lord, you have probed me
And you know me;
You know when I sit and when I stand;
You understand my thoughts from afar.
My journeys and my rest you scrutinize,
With all my ways you are familiar.
Even before a word is on my tongue,
Behold, O Lord, you know the whole of it.
Behind me and before, you hem me in
And rest your hand upon me.

Such knowledge is too wonderful for me
Too lofty for me to attain.
Where can I go from your spirit?
From your presence where can I flee?
If I go up to the heavens, you are there;
If I sink to the nether world,
You are present there.
If I take the wings of the dawn,
If I settle at the farthest limits of the sea,
Even there your hand shall guide me,
And your right hand hold me fast.
If I say, "Surely the darkness shall hide me,
And night shall be my light"-
For you darkness itself is not dark, and night
shines as the day
(darkness and light are the same).
Truly you have formed my inmost being.
You knit me in my mother's womb.
I give thanks that
I am fearfully, wonderfully made;
Wonderful are your works.
My soul also you knew full well;
Nor was my frame unknown to you
When I was made in secret,
When I was fashioned
In the depths of the earth.

Your eyes have seen my actions;
In your book they are all written;
My days were limited
Before one of them existed.
How weighty are your designs, O God;
How vast the sum of them!
Were I to recount them,
They would outnumber the sands;
Did I reach the end of them,
I should still be with you.

HOPE

PSALM 123
To you I lift up my eyes
Who are enthroned in heaven.
Behold, as the eyes of servants
Are on the hands of their masters,
As the eyes of a maid
Are on the hands of her mistress,
So are our eyes on the Lord, our God,
Till he have pity on us.

DISTRESS

PSALM 22
My God, my God,
Why have you forsaken me,
Far from my prayer,
From the words of my cry?
O my God, I cry out by day,
And you answer not;
By night, and there is no relief for me.
Yet you are enthroned in the holy place,
O glory of Israel!
In you our fathers trusted;
They trusted and you delivered them.
To you they cried, and they escaped;
In you they trusted,
And they were not put to shame.
But I am a worm not a man;
The scorn of men, despised by the people.
All who see me scoff at me;
They mock me with parted lips,
They wag their heads:
"He relied on the Lord; let him deliver him,
Let him rescue him, if he loves him."
You have been my guide
Since I was first formed,

My security at my mother's breast.
To you I was committed at birth,
From my mother's womb you are my God.
Be not far from me, for I am in distress;
Be near, for I have no one to help me.

PSALM 31
In you, O Lord, I take refuge;
Let me never be put to shame.
In your justice rescue me,
Incline your ear to me,
Make haste to deliver me!
Be my rock of refuge,
A stronghold to give me safety.
You are my rock and my fortress;
For your name's sake
You will lead me and guide me.
You will free me from the snare
They have set for me
For you are my refuge.
Into your hands I commend my spirit;
You will redeem me,
O Lord, O faithful God.
You hate those who worship vain idols
But my trust is in the Lord.
I will rejoice and be glad of your kindness,

When you have seen my affliction
And watched over me in distress.

SORROW

PSALM 13
How long, O Lord,
Will you utterly forget me?
How long will you hide your face from me?
How long shall I harbor sorrow in my soul,
Grief in my heart day after day?
How long will my enemy triumph over me?
Look , answer me, O Lord, my God!
Give light to my eyes
That I may not sleep in death
Lest my enemy say, "I have overcome him";
Lest my foes rejoice at my downfall
Though I trusted in your kindness.
Let my heart rejoice in your salvation;
Let me sing of the Lord,
"He has been good to me".

ENEMIES

PSALM 143
O Lord, hear my prayer;

Hearken to my pleading in your faithfulness;
In your justice answer me.
And enter not into
The judgement of your servant,
For before you no living man is just.
For the enemy pursues me;
He has crushed my life to the ground;
He has left me dwelling in the dark,
Like those long dead.
And my spirit is faint within me,
My heart within me is appalled.
I remember the days of old;
I meditate on all your doings,
The works of your hands I ponder.
I stretch out my hands to you;
My soul thirsts for you like parched land.
Hasten to answer me, O Lord,
For my spirit fails me.
Hide not your face from me.
Lest I become like those
Who go down into the pit.
At dawn let me hear of your kindness,
For in you I trust.
Show me the way in which I should walk,
For to you I lift up my soul.

Rescue me from my enemies, O Lord, for in
you I hope.

PSALM 30

O Lord, my God
I cried out to you and you healed me.
O Lord, you brought me up
From the netherworld;
You preserved me from among those
Going down into the pit.
Sing praise to the Lord,
You his faithful ones,
And give thanks to his holy name.
For his anger last but a moment;
A lifetime his good will.
At nightfall, weeping enters in,
But with the dawn rejoicing.
You changed my mourning into dancing;
You took off my sackcloth
And clothed me with gladness
That my soul might sing praises
To you without ceasing
O Lord, my God
Forever will I give you thanks

PSALM 31

In you, O Lord, I take refuge;
Let me never be put to shame.
In your justice rescue me,
Incline your ear to me,
Make haste to deliver me!
Be my rock of refuge,
A stronghold to give me safety
You are my rock and my fortress;
For your name's sake
You will lead me and guide me.

Jubilee 2000 A.D.

Operation Sponsor and Spread

Have you used this book and found it
helpful?
Would you like to do something special to
celebrate this great anniversary of the
coming of Our Lord Jesus Christ?
Do you have a few bucks to spare to
celebrate? Why not join
"Operation Sponsor and Spread"
Easy: Pay the publisher for the printing of
copies for you to distribute to your friends
and acquaintances free of charge.
You can have as many as 250 to "2000"
copies printed for you if you pay for printing
only and you give them out to 250 - 2000
people. Use your money wisely to lay up
treasures for yourself that you will be
eternally glad for!!
Besides you may like to put your name in
print as the sponsor so the user can
remember to pray for you.
Don't hesitate, join
"Operation Sponsor and Spread"

**Contact: Akin-Wura Publishers, P.O. Box ~~84186~~,
Chicago, Illinois 60680, U.S.A.**